Söderöra
Blidö
Rödlöga
Åsmansboda
Röder
Svenska
Stenarna
Svartlöga
Lygna
In-Fredel
Ängskär
Skarv
Kallskär
Ut-Fredel
Högfjärden
St. Nassa
Svenska
Högarna
Gillöga
Lökaön
Björkskärs-
fjärden
L. Nassa
Björkskär
Ramsmorön
Horsstens-
fjärden
Horssten
Grönskär
Sandhamn
Almagrundet
0
10
20 km
0
5
10 M
D1693533

SWEDISH SUMMER

RECIPES FROM
THE STOCKHOLM ARCHIPELAGO

Text Viveca Sten
Photography Jeppe Wikström
Food photography Lina Eriksson
Food creator Tove Nilsson
Design Patric Leo
Layout Amelie Stenbeck-Ramel
Editors Marlaine Delargy (text) and Tamara Grace Blom (recipes)
Colour separation Linjepunkt, Falun, Sweden
Printing Livonia Print, Latvia 2015
ISBN 978-91-7126-341-4
www.maxstrom.se

Viveca Sten

SWEDISH SUMMER

RECIPES FROM THE STOCKHOLM ARCHIPELAGO

TRANSLATION BY
KIM AND LUKAS LOUGHRAN

PHOTOGRAPHY JEPPE WIKSTRÖM AND LINA ERIKSSON

BOKFÖRLAGET MAX STRÖM

To my father, who loves the archipelago as much as I do

CONTENTS

WELCOME!

ARCHIPELAGO EATING

When I think of Sandhamn, I always think of food.

Coffee and cakes on the jetty and barbecues at sunset, picnics on granite cliffs, and crayfish parties with home-flavoured *schnapps*.

We eat heartily and often out here in the archipelago. And everything tastes fantastic. That's the way it is.

That doesn't mean everything revolves around food, but we're thinking about it for much of the day, preparing, then enjoying. Nowhere else do I think so hard about what I'm going to eat. And there's a certain thrill about having the time, for once, to plan carefully: What shall we make for dinner?

There's the shopping, chopping, cutting, marinating and grilling. In June, with the scent of the lilacs wafting through the air and the elder trees in bloom, we revel in the flavours of asparagus, beetroot and sugar snap peas tossed in butter. Then I'll whip some cream for the strawberries and add plenty of sugar.

July brings blueberries and currants: you'll find me hunkered down in the blueberry bushes, picking until my fingers are a deep shade of magenta. Sometimes the berries are for a meringue, sometimes just to scatter over the children's favourite—white chocolate pie.

In August, when the air is heavy with the scent of roses, we feast on crayfish or whitefish caught that day, or we just pile vegetables onto the barbecue alongside a chunk of meat.

There's so much delicous food!

Stockholm's archipelago—thirty thousand islands fanning out into the Baltic—is one of the nation's treasures, a sailor's delight and home to a special breed of islanders, but also beloved by tens of thousands of summer guests.

I have many archipelago memories. That balmy July evening on Kalvskär, the little island east of Sandhamn, when we boiled new potatoes in a bucket of seawater on a little gas burner. We cleaned perch

A pilot boat about to dock at Sandhamn. In the distance, the Svängen lighthouse shows where the deep-water channel curves out to sea.

Next page: The Midsummer maypole on Adolfs Torg square in the middle of the village. Hundreds of visitors come every year to celebrate a traditional Midsummer feast, with accordion music and dancing around the maypole.

out on the rocks, and there were sugar snap peas and lettuce from our garden, and a pie made with blueberries from the sparse pine forests of Sandhamn. The sun set slowly into the sea against a backdrop of pink sky and the silhouette of the Grönskär lighthouse. A magical evening.

Food also contributes to friendship and a sense of community. There have been many delightful meals with neighbours and friends over the years. Breakfasts on the jetty in bathrobes or swimsuits, long, lazy lunches followed by a short siesta—dozing in the afternoon sun is wonderful.

Since we live in a rustic idyll, fifty metres from granddad's garden and thirty from where our cousins live, we often gather for cross-generational dinners.

Mostly, we share cooking duties. Somebody makes a salad and boils the potatoes, somebody else barbecues or smokes the fish. Often fish we've caught ourselves, accompanied by tasty treats picked or harvested from the vegetable garden. I'm often the one who does the dessert—I've always had a weakness for delicious pies and generous meringues.

I love those warm summer evenings when the smell of steak and baked potatoes fills the air, when the barbecue sizzles and the sparks dance away. Swallows fly high overhead, and the sound of laughter drifts across from nearby gardens.

A little later, we'll go down to the jetty to sit while the tiny tots play

Sandhamn has always attracted writers and artists, and almost every garden has something artistic to show off.

Steamboats were serving Sandhamn as early as the 1860s—at the time, this was a revolution for the islanders, who had previously had no choice but to row or sail to reach the capital city of Stockholm.

in the shingle. If we're lucky, the teenagers will hang around for a while after dinner before heading off to other hunting grounds.

My children are fifth-generation Sandhamn summer residents, and my father has been here for eighty years.

Some of my best Sandhamn memories are from meals just like these, sitting beneath a sky turning orange-red as the sun slowly sets. The bay is so still it looks like purple silk, the islands seem to float on the shimmering water.

Moments of pure happiness.

I just love strolling along Sandhamn's western shore. My first impulse to write crime novels came while walking here. What if I were to find a body washed up by the waves …

I'm not the only one who loves cooking in the Stockholm archipelago. In this book I visit like-minded people on other islands, peeking into their kitchen cupboards and eating their food.

Those who have generously shared their best recipes are Janne on Bullerö island, Eva and Klara on Södermöja, Erik on Harö, Fredrik on Grönskär, Magdalena on Lygna and Sarah out on Svenska Högarna.

We've got everything from picnics to lazy lunches and fancy dinners. I've been treated to a seductive fish stew, tasted irresistible fillet of lamb and enjoyed a delicious summer cake, just to mention a few.

I've also baked all my favourites and picked up some islander tips that I'm happy to share.

You are all welcome to join me and my friends in the archipelago to sample some delicious food.

SANDHAMN COFFEE BREAK

"ARE YOU AT HOME?"

"We're on a boat, on our way! Are you at home this afternoon?"
Living on Sandhamn, we get this a lot. When you wake up in the morning, you've no idea who might come calling in just a few hours. There is no lack of spontaneous visits, sometimes with just a text message to alert you.

"*We're right here, in the harbour* ☺"

Sometimes as one set of guests is leaving, others are arriving. Sometimes they turn up together, adults and teenagers, children and friends of friends. There's a constant flow in the summer, and at times I'm almost tempted to rename our summer cottage "Sten's Guesthouse".

So it's a good idea to keep a stock of buns and cakes handy; you never know how many cups you'll need to set out.

My great-grandfather Oscar came to Sandhamn in 1917 and bought our family home, built close to the water by a master pilot. Islanders had mocked the old sea captain—why build where it's windiest? He stuck it out for three years, then along came my great-grandfather.

Oscar saw a handsome archipelago house by the water with a sunset view. And he got it for a song, by his reckoning.

The pilot was happy. He had conned a naïve Stockholmer into buying a draughty house some distance outside the village. And he had been handsomely paid, more than the place was worth, by his reckoning.

Everyone was satisfied, and ever since, the family has spent every single summer on Sandhamn.

Just boarding the ferry that will take us to the island makes me happy. We're on our way! My heart sings as soon as we spot the narrow straits with the red-painted houses, the white buoys bobbing off the jetties.

The little island is out on the edge of the archipelago, with less than a hundred permanent residents. However, it's a vibrant community with shops, an inn, a big hotel and even a day care centre. The small general store sells food and takes orders for wine and spirits and medicines.

Sandhamn has no cars, so consequently there are more bicycles and carts. I've used our old trolley for everything from food and luggage to children and pets. In the background looms the old pilots' lookout, once manned around the clock.

Next page: Is anything more delightful than afternoon coffee on the veranda with good friends? The old-fashioned windows almost make it feel like we're outdoors. This is my very favourite spot in the house..

It is also our improvised ATM, dispensing cash on credit. Ferries ply back and forth to the mainland at least four times a day, even in winter.

But summer is when Sandhamn really comes alive, with three thousand summer residents and over a hundred thousand visitors.

Sandhamn—strictly speaking only the name of the harbour on the island of Sandön (Sandy island)—is the most popular destination in the Stockholm archipelago. It's the only island on a sandy rather than rock base, in contrast to the other thirty thousand islands.

In the summer months the harbour area is crammed with boats, the big hotel is fully booked and the outdoor cafés are always busy. Tourists flock to the shallow beaches at Trouville on the southeast side, where the waters are warm and the sand white. In the evenings the smell of cooking drifts through the air as people barbecue in gardens and on boats.

There is no doubt that this is an island for socialising; it's perfect for getting together over food. Which takes us back to where we started.

"Are you at home this afternoon?"

When guests arrive, we almost always start with the classic Swedish *fika*, or coffee break. It's part of the Sandhamn culture.

If we're lucky there's time to bake buns and a sponge cake, otherwise we improvise, maybe by spreading whipped cream on a leftover cake, topping it with fresh raspberries and calling it a "summer surprise".

Over the years I've learnt how to be partly prepared at all times: I store bags of risen but *unbaked* buns in the freezer, thaw them for about an hour, pop them in the oven and hey presto! Freshly baked buns! A bake-off, home-style.

Another trick is to keep a bag of crisprolls in the kitchen cupboard; they're tasty and have a sort of summer feel. They'll keep forever if stored dry.

But I prefer a little warning, since I really love to bake and put on a proper spread. It's so much fun to have an old-fashioned afternoon tea with lots of luscious treats: buns with blueberry filling, chocolate roly

The old boatsheds contain all kinds of things: fishing nets, battered oars, tools and equipment that might someday come in handy. Everything but the kitchen sink.

Next page: The harbour at Sandhamn—or Sandön, the island's formal name—used to be filled with sailing ships waiting for favourable winds to take them towards the capital city. The island was not properly settled until the 17th century when the king commanded the farmers on nearby Eknö island to man a pilot station.

poly with Swedish *punsch* or rum cream, or a pie made with fresh berries. Sometimes we'll have it on the covered veranda, sometimes down by the jetty with the waves rolling in.

When the table is laid with coffee cups, cake stands, pastries, buns and biscuits, my soul is at rest.

But I have to be on my guard; if I turn my back for just a minute to fetch the coffee, the seagulls will attack. Given the slightest chance, they dive at the plate and grab something. Off they fly, contentedly screeching, with a bun or two in their beaks.

And who can blame them? It's all so tasty!

5

BLUEBERRY BUNS

Makes 20 buns:
100 g / ¼ lb butter
4 dl / 1 ⅔ cups whole milk
1 tsp ground cardamom seeds
1 dl / ⅖ cup sugar
a pinch of salt
25 g / 1 oz fresh yeast or
2 ½ tsp active dried yeast
approx. 10 dl / 4 ¼ cups plain flour (600 g / 1 ⅓ lb)

Filling:
250 g / ½ lb marzipan
225 g / ½ lb blueberries (4–5 dl / 1½–2 cups)
½ dl / 3 tbsp sugar

1 egg for glazing

Picking blueberries makes me calm. It's almost like meditating, sitting among the blueberry shrubs and picking until my fingers turn purple. I like to have earphones and listen to an audiobook or the radio. Afterwards I'll make divine blueberry buns with almond paste to round off the taste and deliver sweetness.

You can deep-freeze these buns but they're best freshly baked.

Here's how

1. Melt the butter and add the milk, cardamom, sugar and salt. Heat to a tepid 37C/100F. Crumble the yeast into a bowl and pour the liquid over. Stir to dissolve the yeast.
2. Mix in most of the flour and stir until you get a smooth dough. Add more flour if needed. Shape into a roll and let it rise under a clean tea towel for about 40 minutes.
3. Cut the marzipan into 20 thin slices. If the roll is too thick cut it lengthwise before slicing. The slices should be 5cm/2in in diameter.
4. Heat the oven to 225C/440F. Put the dough on a flour-dusted work surface and cut in two halves. Divide each half into 10 equal pieces. Knead them into balls and press flat onto a baking tray lined with parchment paper.
5. Stick a slice of marzipan into each bun, making a cavity. Spoon a tbsp of blueberries into the cavity on top of the almond paste. Sprinkle the blueberries with sugar and let the buns rise for another 25 minutes.
6. Glaze the edges with egg wash and bake the buns in the middle of the oven for about 12 minutes.

LEMON MUFFINS

Makes 12 muffins:
125 g / ¼ lb butter, room temperature
1 ½ dl / ⅔ cup sugar
2 large eggs
1 tsp vanilla sugar
1 dl / ⅖ cup milk
3 dl /1 ¼ cups plain flour
1 ½ tsp baking powder
1 lemon, grated zest and juice from ½ lemon
whipped cream, strawberries

Muffins are a lifesaver when you're pressed for time. They take barely a quarter of an hour to mix, and another to bake. You can't ask for better than that. And strawberries and whipped cream make them really fancy.

If I'm in a big, big hurry, I skip the lemon and mix in 2–3 tbsp of cocoa instead. There's nothing wrong with chocolate muffins. Those are best served with raspberries.

Here's how

1. Preheat the oven to 180C/355F. Use an electric whisk and whip the butter and the sugar for about 5 minutes.
2. Mix in one egg at a time then add vanilla, sugar and milk into a smooth batter.
3. Mix the flour with the baking powder and add to the batter. Grate the lemon zest and squeeze half of the fruit and add to the mix.
4. Pour the batter into muffin cases filling to ⅔ and bake in the middle of the oven for about 15 minutes.
5. When serving, garnish with strawberries and a dollop of whipped cream.

SWEDISH CHOCOLATE "BISCOTTI"

Makes 30 biscotti:
2 dl / 4/5 cup sugar
1 egg
tbsp vanilla sugar
tbsp cocoa
200 g / ½ lb butter
5 dl / 2 cups plain flour
1 ½ tsp baking powder
1 dl / 2/5 cup finely
chopped almonds

My children adore my chocolate "biscotti" and so do I! They're crunchy and you're soon reaching for another. They can be stored in a cake tin—practical when visitors might be on their way. That's the way it goes in Sandhamn.

Here's how

1. Preheat the oven to 225C/440F. Whisk together sugar, egg, vanilla sugar and cocoa.
2. Melt the butter and let it cool before adding it.
3. Mix the flour and baking powder and sift into the batter, stirring to make a dough.
4. On a baking tray lined with parchment paper, shape the dough into three logs. Flatten the logs. Make sure that they aren't too close together since they will expand.
5. Sprinkle over the almonds and bake for 10 minutes in the middle of the oven.
6. Cut the logs diagonally into oblongs while still hot and soft.

CHOCOLATE & RUM ROLY POLY

Makes 1 roly poly (approximately 12 pieces):
3 eggs
1½ dl / ⅔ cup sugar (for the batter)
2 dl / ⅘ cup sugar (to dust the baking paper)
2 dl / ⅘ cup flour
1tsp baking powder
4 tbsp cocoa powder

Filling:
75 g / 2 ½ oz butter, room temperature
1 ½ dl / ⅔ cup icing sugar
1 tsp vanilla sugar
1 egg yolk
1–2 tbsp Swedish punsch (similar to arak) or dark rum

Garnish:
cocoa powder
icing sugar

My chocolate & rum roly poly melts in your mouth and the old-fashioned rum taste triggers summer associations for Swedes.

Some people think roly polys are hard to make but in fact using baking paper makes the rolling part easy. I serve this for afternoon tea or coffee but also, with lightly whipped cream, as a dessert.

Here's how

1. Preheat the oven to 225C/440F.
2. Start with the base: Using an electric whisk, beat the eggs and 1½ dl / ⅔ cup of the sugar until porous. Mix flour, cocoa powder and baking powder and sift it into the batter. Stir until smooth.
3. Spread out onto a baking tray lined with a sheet of baking paper. Bake in the middle of the oven for about 5 minutes. Let cool.
4. Filling: Whip the butter, icing sugar and vanilla sugar until porous. Add the punsch (or dark rum) drop by drop as you continue whipping. This minimises the risk of the cream splitting.
5. Turn the base upside down onto another sheet of baking paper dusted with 2 dl/⅘ cup of sugar. Carefully detach the baking paper.
6. Gently spread the cream onto the cooled but not yet cold base. Roll it up.
7. Let the cake set in the baking paper for a few hours. Dust with cocoa powder and icing sugar before serving.

BANANA NUT CAKE

Makes 1 cake (approximately 12 pieces):
2 dl / ⅘ cup sugar
1 dl / ⅖ cup rapeseed/ vegetable oil
2 eggs
1 tsk vanilla sugar
3 dl / 1 ¼ cups plain flour
½ tsp salt
1 tsp baking powder
½ tsp cinnamon
1 dl / ⅖ cup grated zucchini or carrot
1 dl / ⅖ cup ground hazelnuts or walnuts
1 dl / ⅖ cup mashed banana

Frosting:
100 g / ¼ lb cream cheese
75 g / 2 ½ oz butter, room temperature
2 ½ dl / 1 cup icing sugar
1 ½ tsp vanilla sugar

Optional: 1 dl / ⅖ cup chopped nuts

I learned to bake this when I was an exchange student in the United States. We used nuts, vegetables and oil. Different, but very tasty.

This cake is dense and moist, and perfect for the lactose-intolerant because it uses oil instead of butter. It's great for picnics since it doesn't crumble like ordinary sponge cake does.

Here's how

1. Preheat the oven to 175C/350F.
2. Beat the sugar, oil and egg whites until porous. Mix all the dry ingredients and add to the batter.
3. Combine the grated vegetable, nuts and mashed banana and carefully fold into the batter.
4. Pour into a pan (approximately 20×20cm/8×8in) that has been greased and dusted with bread crumbs. Bake in the middle of the oven for about 30 minutes. Let cool.
5. Beat all the frosting ingredients with an electric whisk and frost the cake before serving. If desired, top with chopped nuts.

WHITE CHOCOLATE PIE WITH BLUEBERRIES

Makes approximately 8 portions:
Crust:
100 g / ¼ lb butter or margarine
3 dl / 1 ¼ cups plain flour
½ dl / ¼ cup icing sugar
2–3 tbsp cold water
a pinch of salt

Filling:
3 dl / 1 ¼ cups whipping cream
100 g / ¼ lb white chocolate
2 egg yolks
2 dl / ⅘ cup blueberries, fresh or frozen

White chocolate has a fine, mild taste and can upgrade most recipes. The blueberries are embedded in a hearty chocolate mousse that caresses the tongue. Not exactly a low-calories treat, but irresistibly good. If you don't have blueberries, strawberries will do just fine.

Here's how

1. Cut the butter into small cubes and place all the crust ingredients in a bowl or food processor and combine until you get a ball. No kneading!
2. Roll or press the dough into a pie plate about 24cm/10in in diameter. Prick the bottom with a fork. Chill in the fridge for at least 30 minutes.
3. Heat the oven to 225C/440F. Bake the crust on the middle rack for 10–15 minutes. Let cool.
4. Filling: Whip the cream. Break the chocolate and melt it in a bowl over boiling water (bain marie). Remove from the heat.
5. Fold the chocolate into the cream. Beat the egg yolks and fold in with a spatula.
6. Spread the mousse in the pie crust. Let it set for no less than 30 minutes. Garnish with blueberries just before serving.

Tip

For a crispier pie: After pre-baking the crust, brush with 50 g / 2 oz of melted chocolate. Chill in the fridge so the chocolate sets before adding the filling.

BULLERÖ

FOOD TALK ON AN ARTIST'S ISLAND

Bullerö is half an hour by boat to the south of Sandhamn. Just as we round the point that protects the little harbour, it strikes me that this is exactly the same view that greeted some of Sweden's greatest painters—Bruno Liljefors, Anders Zorn, Albert Engström and all the other members of the "Bullerö gang" at the beginning of the twentieth century.

Bruno Liljefors had a hunting lodge built in the Bullerö skerries—it became a studio as much as a hunting lodge. Liljefors never tired of painting the scenery. The Bullerö gang would feast under the light summer night sky and not head home until all the food and drink was gone.

I am standing on the jetty thinking about all this when along comes the person I'm here to meet. He's Janne Olsén, the nature reserve ranger for Bullerö island.

Janne is a big man, a robust ex-naval officer who watches over Bullerö with a keen eye and a firm hand, and a deep feeling for the archipelago. His greying beard is as thick as the hair on his head and the pockets of his blue dungarees are filled with all sorts of things—a pocket-knife, a screwdriver, keys to various cottages on the island.

We sit in the sun in front of the red-painted wooden cottage that is the ranger's residence and talk about favourite summer dishes.

"Fresh cod, fried within hours of catching it," offers Janne, leaning forward as he warms to the subject: "And new potatoes boiled in seawater, served with just plain butter. Or baked whitefish—I stuff it with all kinds of delicious things: red onion, butter, parsley and sea salt. Oh, the smell when you open the oven door a fraction to check if it's ready! There's nothing better!"

We talk about the cod population in the Baltic, which seems to be recovering, but turbot is increasingly rare. "Fried turbot with grated horseradish and potatoes boiled with dill. Could anything be better than that?" enthuses Janne.

As we chat, the island chickens come to call, pecking interestedly

The flag flies in front of the 18th-century house that is Janne Olsén's home. The other building is part of the hostel complex for lucky tourists, but you need to book early!

around our legs and flapping their wings. Their russet feathers gleam in the sun. Not far off, a five-year-old boy watches from behind the tourist hostel fence. Will he pluck up the courage to come over and pet the chickens?

After a while, a rooster graces us with his presence, a fine specimen, impressively ruffling his feathers. But he's slightly lazy, according to Janne, who has to wake the bird in the mornings.

"I usually get up at six, and he's still sleeping."

The sun blazes down, there is no wind and hardly a ripple on the sea. In front of us, a long walkway leads over the rocks to where the boats tie up. From the end of the dock, you can see a small sauna across the bay.

Behind the sauna's tiled roof is a grey cliff, a smooth stone wall protecting bathers from the wind, so they can still relax outdoors with their cold beers after their sauna. Heating the sauna takes a couple of hours, but it's well worth it. When the sauna is being used in winter, the smell of wood smoke drifts across the water.

We get up and wander over what were once potato fields. A flock of sheep approaches, attracted by the contents of Janne's yellow bucket.

Suddenly I am surrounded by ewes and lambs butting and shoving; a smooth mouth nudges my hand, trying to get at the last of the grain in my palm. The little lamb's ears poke straight out, and even though its fleece is grey and curly, its head is covered in wispy brown hair.

When we leave, the sheep follow us up to the narrow path that runs through the village. I wave goodbye to my little lamb.

A huge maple shades the path between the red 18th-century houses that are now the tourist hostel. Janne's property is the only one with a fence around it. "Without it, I wouldn't have any flowers left," he says apologetically.

We stroll northward, to Bruno Liljefors's hunting lodge. The brown log cabin stands alone in what was once a small inlet. Rising land means the water is now about twenty metres away, and the mouth of the inlet

The world's sleepiest rooster? On Bullerö island, Janne wakes the rooster, not the other way round.

Sheep and lambs graze in the grassy hollow behind Hemviken village. The animals are completely unafraid and tag along happily with visitors.

is overgrown with clumps of tall reeds. But you can see for miles, and the sea is smooth and calm outside the windows.

The old artists seem to whisper on the wind. I imagine I can smell turpentine and hear the sigh of a brush on canvas.

A few hundred metres from here is the Bridal Path, a stairway built of rough boulders, leading up to a flat area of smooth rock alternating with soft moss. Creeping juniper and crowberry grow in the cracks between the rocks. Rainwater has collected in small pools.

A spider's web stretches across a deep crack, forming a perfect pattern in its fragility. But the spider is nowhere to be seen.

It is completely still and quiet, and I remain standing at the edge of the cliff for a long time. I close my eyes and try to imagine how it must feel to get married beneath a blue sky with nothing but the sea lapping alongside. How wonderful it would be with lambs gambolling around and a sumptuous wedding feast waiting in the old hunting lodge, perhaps with Janne's amazing summer cake as a finale.

A joy to both the soul and the stomach. Just in the spirit of Bruno Liljefors.

There were frequent feasts in Bruno Liljefors' old hunting lodge, the guests often not leaving until the food and drink were finished. In between, the famous artist found time to paint.

Four shades of blue. On a beautiful summer's day, sailing boats glide over the smooth surface.

Next page: Over nine hundred islets comprise the Bullerö skerries, which are partly a protected nature reserve. Bruno Liljefors sold the main island in 1923. Today, Bullerö and its closest islands are owned by the Swedish state.

BOUILLABAISSE À LA BULLERÖ

Makes 4 portions:
800 g / 1 ¾ lb cod, whitefish, trout, zander or perch
6 allspice berries
2 white peppercorns
1 leek
4 carrots
3 tbsp coarsely chopped dill
3 tbsp finely chopped chives
½ red onion, finely chopped
sourdough bread
salt
freshly ground black pepper

Robust fish dishes are traditional among archipelago folks and new kinds are constantly being invented—the principle being, use what you've got.

A full-bodied white wine or a lager beer with a schnapps chaser work beautifully with this stew.

Here's how

1. Gut and fillet the fish. Put the heads and all the bones in a large pot and cover with 1 litre/2 pints of water. Add the allspice and peppercorns. Reduce on low heat until only half the liquid remains. Discard the bones and strain into a new pot. (In a hurry? Use store-bought fish cubes.)
2. Clean and cut the leek into thin strips. Peel and cut the carrot into coins. Add the vegetables, herbs and onions to the stock. Bring to a boil and let simmer for a few minutes. Season with salt and pepper.
3. Cut the fish into bite size pieces and put in the pot. Simmer for another 5 minutes.
4. Serve with toasted sourdough bread.

GRILLED LAMB RACKS

Serves 4:
1.2 kg / 2 ½ lb lamb racks
2 tbsp Chinese soy sauce
2 tbsp balsamic vinegar
1 ½ tbsp honey
1 tbsp finely chopped rosemary
salt
freshly ground black pepper

Barbecued lamb is so good that I get a happy buzz every time I smell it. And it's a refreshing change from the beef and pork that so dominate summer barbecues.

These marinated lamb racks together with grilled onions and a tasty potato salad make a feast.

Here's how

1. Combine soy, vinegar, honey and rosemary for the marinade. Pour in a plastic bag with the meat and leave for at least 2 hours.
2. Remove the meat from the bag, saving the marinade.
3. Season the meat with salt and pepper.
4. Grill it on all sides for about 30 minutes. If you can check the core temperature, the meat is done at 60C/140F.
5. Baste the meat with the marinade while cooking. Serve the lamb right from the grill.

ARCHIPELAGO PORK FILLET AND KABANOS

Serves 4:
600 g / 1 ⅓ lb pork loin/fillet
3 spicy sausages
e.g. chorizo or kabanos
4 carrots
2 red onions
1 zucchini or small squash
olive oil
salt
freshly ground black pepper
3 tbsp finely chopped
chives or parsley

The muurikka, originally Finnish, is a flat, cast-iron griddle pan, and a great tool if you love cooking outdoors. It can be used over an open fire or a primus stove. The wide surface provides plenty of room for both meat and veg. And everything is done in a flash—the food almost cooks itself!

Accompany this rustic dish with a full-bodied red wine.

Here's how

1. Cut the meat and sausages into large chunks. Peel the carrots and onions. Cut all the vegetables into medium size pieces.
2. Place the muurikka over an open fire or heat it with a gas burner.
3. Cook the meat and sausages in the oil until thoroughly cooked, turning them often.
4. Add the vegetables (not including the chives and parsley) and give it all a good stir until everything is hot. Season with salt and pepper. Toss in the chives or parsley and serve.

GRILLED WHOLE PERCH

Serves 4:
4 perches
100 g / ¼ lb butter
2 tbsp finely chopped dill
2 tbsp finely chopped parsley
2 tbsp finely chopped chives
sea salt
freshly ground black pepper
1 lemon

Could anything be easier?

Before putting the perch in the oven, fill it with a few generous bits of butter, fresh herbs and a good onion—or anything else that will add to the taste. Don't be stingy with the filling—go big! Then sit back and enjoy.

Here's how

1. Preheat the oven to 150C/300F. Gut and rinse the fish thoroughly.
2. Put the fish on an oven tray and fill the cavity with herbs and chunks of butter. Season with salt and pepper. Place a half lemon on the tray to squeeze over the fish when it's done.
3. Cook the fish in the middle of the oven for 25–30 minutes.
4. Serve immediately, accompanied with dill, steamed new potatoes and a salad. A dab of parsley butter heightens the taste. A well-chilled white wine or lager beer is an excellent accompaniment.

JANNE'S SUMMER CAKE

Makes 1 cake (approximately 10 pieces) :
Cake base:
4 eggs
2 dl / ⁴⁄₅ cup sugar
1 dl / ²⁄₅ cup plain flour
1 dl / ²⁄₅ cup potato starch
1 tsp baking powder

Filling:
1 tbsp Cointreau
2 dl / ⁴⁄₅ cup raspberry jam, preferably homemade
5 dl / 2 ¹⁄₅ cups whipping cream
1 ½ punnet strawberries

A fail-proof, super-easy summer cake. Its secret is the splash of Cointreau that rounds off the filling. Be generous with strawberries and cream and you can't go wrong. Fresh coffee or homemade lemonade makes your coffee break complete.

Here's how

1. Preheat the oven to 175C/345F. Grease a springform pan, about 24cm/10in in diameter and dust it with bread crumbs.
2. Beat the eggs and sugar until porous. In a separate bowl combine flour and baking powder. Sift the dry ingredients into the batter and swiftly stir with a spatula until smooth.
3. Pour the batter into the pan and bake in the middle of the oven for about 35 minutes. Let the cake cool and cut into three discs.
4. Brush the discs with Cointreau. Layer the cake with raspberry jam, whipped cream and mashed strawberries. Garnish the top with halved strawberries. Put the cake in the fridge for about an hour to let it absorb everything.

SÖDERMÖJA

MOTHER AND DAUGHTER COOKING

After the rugged skerries of the outer archipelago, Södermöja feels like a warm, welcoming embrace. Rounding the little island of Byholmen, we are met by lush greenery and mature oak trees, with an old merchant's villa on the point, showing the way.

Södermöja is an island on its own, separated from Stora Möja by the Möja Ström channel.

Möja (taking the two islands of Södermöja and Stora Möja together) has been populated since the days of the Vikings and is a bustling archipelago community with almost three hundred year-round residents, a school and a daily ferry service.

My mouth starts watering as soon as I enter the Ejemyr home, a yellow turn of the century house—there is a delicious smell of barbecued lamb. Möja used to export strawberries to the mainland, but now that the strawberry farms have gone out of business, rearing lambs is becoming popular.

"Lamb is Möja's new strawberry," says Eva Ejemyr, chopping lettuce in the kitchen. Her youngest daughter, Klara, brings in tomatoes from the vine on the terrace. They are warm from the sun and she cups them in her hand as though they were nestlings.

There are pots of herbs everywhere, and a big bunch of rhubarb lies on a work surface, waiting to be turned into a compote. A generous ceramic bowl is filled with peaches, apricots, apples and cherries.

In the evening, the old kerosene lamp above the kitchen table will be lit. It is a faithful old servant, just like the white tiled stove in the corner and the stove's sisters in the other rooms. It's sunny today, but when the north wind blows and the rain comes bucketing down, lighting a fire chases away the damp.

The house is set on a hillside, which is why the kitchen is on the upper level. There is a panoramic view, and I see through the windows that the wind has freshened. It's gusting now, and the water is visibly choppy.

The table is laid for a feast in the little pavilion on the hillside, about ten metres above the house we're in. There are "only" six people for

Eva prepares dessert and coffee in the pretty pavilion up on the hill. The Swedish flag flies proudly outside.

Eva and Klara Ejemyr, mother and daughter, creating in the kitchen they love so much—chopping, cutting and laughing with as much energy as enthusiasm.

lunch today—sometimes it's a dozen, sometimes up to twenty, counting all the children and grandchildren.

The flagpole flies the Swedish colours, blue and yellow, and the pennant is almost horizontal in the brisk wind. Snug in our sheltered corner, we tuck into wild garlic pesto and fillet of lamb.

When we've almost finished, Eva leans back in her chair, smiling contentedly as she spreads a dab of pesto on a lukewarm chunk of potato. The pale green blends perfectly with the light yellow of the new potato.

"Something about the archipelago creates prime conditions for cooking," she says, reaching for another potato. "Everything tastes so good out here."

Klara gives her mother's arm an affectionate squeeze and her brown curls bounce in the afternoon light. In her pretty 1940s-style dress she looks like a character from an old black-and-white movie, but Klara describes herself as a genuine archipelago kid. She was a cook on board the ferry steamer Norrskär; she also started the Möja tourist office, and ran a catering business with Eva.

Reminiscing, they laugh at the memory of a wedding with eighty guests. The preparations went without a hitch, but just as they served eighty portions of a main course they had somehow managed to get ready all at the same time, the toastmaster tapped his glass. The hot food slowly cooled while a guest gave an apparently endless speech.

"I wanted to scream at him to shut up and start eating!" admits Klara.

The mouth-watering mud cake served with finely sliced strawberries is so good that I let every bite linger in my mouth. I take another spoonful, then another, enjoying the tastes blending on my palate: dark chocolate, freshly brewed coffee, fresh strawberries and smooth cream.

A little later, Eva and Klara show me what might well be the prettiest kitchen garden on the island. It belongs to the Hägerö family and they look after their plants with endless love. Their care is visible in the green leaves in the meticulously tended beds. Not a single weed can be seen among the lettuce, leeks and cucumbers. Rosemary and thyme grow in regimented lines and further off, I notice some asparagus.

Wild strawberries have their own corner and the crimson fruit, already ripe, is irresistible. I can't help picking a few, and suddenly old memories rise to the surface: I'm six years-old, gathering wild strawberries with my grandmother. Grandma hands me a blade of grass and shows me how to string the berries onto it. I can still remember my joy when I did it for the first time! On the way back, Eva climbs onto her red quad bike, a blessing when aching knees make long walks impossible.

We say goodbye, but before I leave I am given a small jar of wild garlic pesto to take home. When no one is looking, I open it and dab a little on my finger, just because it's so delicious. The green mixture melts on my tongue and I only wish I had a lukewarm chunk of potato to go with it. When we cast off from Södermöja, Eva and Klara are sitting on the jetty waving goodbye, still in their kitchen aprons.

A quad bike is a great help when Eva's troublesome knees make walking a pain. This time, Klara drove me.

Both strawberries and wild strawberries thrive in this most beautiful of kitchen gardens. The lovingly built stone wall shows how carefully the plants are cared for. It's a sheltered oasis in the wind-swept islands.

TRUFFLE-BAKED BLACK SALSIFY

Makes 4–6 portions:
1 kg / 2 ¼ lb black salsify
water + squeezed lemon
1 tbsp olive oil
1 tsp truffle oil
1 dl red lentils
1 tart apple
300 g / ⅔ lb chanterelles
butter for frying
fresh thyme

Dressing:
2 tbsp olive oil
1 tbsp apple cider vinegar
1 tsp Dijon mustard
1 tsp honey
salt
freshly ground black pepper

Salsify is a little tricky to work with but you get your reward when it lands on your tongue. Delicious truffle oil and the tart apple are seductively good with the chantarelle mushrooms. This dish could turn me into a vegetarian …

Here's how

1. Preheat the oven to 200C/390F. Peel the salsify under a cold tap. To keep it white, dunk the salsify in the lemon water immediately.
2. Transfer it to a heatproof dish and toss with a tbsp of olive oil. Drizzle over with truffle oil. Roast in the middle of the oven for about 30 minutes.
3. For the dressing, combine the olive oil, vinegar, mustard and honey. Season with salt and pepper.
4. Boil the lentils in stock or broth according to the instructions on the packet. Drain and mix with the dressing. Sauté the chanterelles in butter, and season with salt and pepper. Peel and dice the apple.
5. Top the salsify with the lentils, the chanterelles, diced apple and thyme.

NETTLE SOUP

Serves 4:
2 litres/8 cups freshly picked nettles
1 shallot onion
pinch of fennel seeds
butter for frying
1 litre/4 cups water
3 tbsp vegetable stock
1 ½ dl / ⅔ cup cream
salt
freshly ground black pepper
2 tbsp cornstarch + 4 tbsp cold water
2 hardboiled eggs

When I was little we used to pick nettles near Sjösala common, where my grandmother had a summer cottage—delicate green shoots that grandma put in her saucepan. I remember the thrill of picking them, always a little scared I would get stung. But I never did.

Here's how

1. Wash and clean the nettles. Blanch the nettles by immersing them in boiling water for 2 minutes. Rinse immediately under cold water.
2. Peel and chop the onion finely. Carefully sauté the onion and fennel seeds in butter in a pot. Pour in the water and the stock and let boil for about 3 minutes.
3. Add the nettles to the pot. Using a stick mixer, blend the soup until smooth. Add the cream and season with salt and pepper. Dissolve the cornstarch in water and add it to thicken the soup. Serve with the halved eggs.

GRILLED LEG OF LAMB

Serves 6–8:
1 leg of lamb, approx. 2 ½ kg / 5 ½ lb
½ dl / ¼ cup fresh rosemary
½ dl / ¼ cup fresh thyme
2 tbsp olive oil
5 cloves of garlic, crushed
salt
freshly ground black pepper

Lamb roast makes me think of cosy Sunday dinners in the kitchen with all the family. Here, the barbecue does the work. And it's just as much fun to eat outdoors.

The choice of root vegetables is improvised—use what you've got.

Here's how

1. Crush the fresh herbs using a mortar and pestle, add the olive oil, garlic, salt and pepper. Rub the meat with the herb mix. Let the lamb rest with the herbs at room temperature for an hour or so before cooking.
2. Place the lamb in the center of the grill without open flame beneath. Cover the grill with the lid. Use a meat thermometer and cook to the core is 60C/140F (about 1½–2 hours) Wrap in tinfoil and let the meat rest for 15 minutes before carving.
3. Serve with roasted root vegetables such as parsnip, carrot, celeriac and potato and a few colourful salsas (see page 66).

THREE GREAT SWEDISH SALSAS

BEETROOT SALSA WITH RINDÖ CHEESE
250 g / ½ lb beetroot
50 g / 2 oz The Rindö cheese maker's white or substitute with brie
2 tbsp oil
salt
freshly ground pepper

CARROT SALSA WITH SUNFLOWER SEEDS
250 g / ½ lb carrots
½ dl / ¼ cup sunflower seeds
1 ½ dl / ⅔ cup coconut milk
½ fresh red chili, chopped finely
1 clove of garlic, chopped finely
salt
freshly ground pepper

CELERIAC SALSA WITH TRUFFLE OIL
300 g / ⅔ lb celeriac
3 dl / 1 ¼ cups cream
1 dash truffle oil
1 tsp lemon juice
salt

Tasty salsas is a fantastic way to enhance a meal. Everyone likes a flavourful salsa with some nice bread. But be careful your guests don't ruin their appetite before the main course!

Here's how

Beetroot salsa with Rindö cheese:
Boil the beetroot in lightly salted water. Peel and cut into chunks. Using a food processor, blend the beetroot, cheese and oil into a semi-smooth salsa. Season with salt and pepper.

Carrot salsa with sunflower seeds:
Peel and chop the carrots. Roast the sunflower seeds in a dry frying pan. Boil the carrots in the coconut milk with the chili, garlic and salt. Drain the carrots, reserving the liquid, and blend them in a food processor together with half of the sunflower seeds. If needed, adjust the consistency with the coconut milk. Season with salt and pepper. If desired, use the rest of the sunflower seeds to garnish.

Celeriac salsa with truffle oil:
Peel and dice the celeriac and place it in a pot. Pour over cream so it just about covers. Carefully boil the celeriac until tender. Drain, and reserve the cream. Blend in a food processor until smooth using the cream to adjust the thickness. Season with truffle oil, lemon juice, salt and pepper to taste.

WILD GARLIC PESTO

Makes approximately 3 dl / 1 ¼ cups:
100 g / ¼ lb wild garlic
½ dl / ¼ cup sunflower seeds
1 dl / ⅖ cup grated Parmesan cheese
2 dl / ⅘ cup rapeseed oil
1 tsp lemon juice
salt
freshly ground black pepper

Wild garlic pesto is a great alternative to standard basil pesto. The taste is smoother, almost dulcet, but oh so good! Sometimes I spread my pesto on half a cooled new potato. It will literally melt in your mouth.

Here's how

1. Wash the wild garlic and dry carefully. Using either a food processor or a stick mixer blend the wild garlic, sunflower seeds and Parmesan cheese with half the oil. Add oil to get the desired consistency.
2. Season with lemon juice, salt and pepper. Pour the pesto into a clean jar and cover the surface with oil (so it will keep).

LAMB IN DILL

Serves 4–6:
2 yellow onions
3 carrots
1 kg / 2 ¼ lb stewing lamb, e.g. shoulder, blade or breast
12 dl / 5 cups water
2 bay leaves
5 white peppercorns
2 ½ tbsp butter
2 ½ tbsp plain flour
1 ½ dl / ⅔ cup thick cream
1 tbsp lemon juice
2 tsp sugar
salt
freshly ground black pepper
½ dl / ¼ cup finely chopped fresh dill

Lamb and dill are two great tastes that get even better when bonded in a stew. When the Swedish summer turns cold and rainy, a tangy, slightly old-fashioned meat stew with dill is a real comfort. New potatoes make a great side dish.

Here's how

1. Peel the onions and carrots. Cut the onions into wedges and the carrots into "coins". Clean and cut the meat into cubes about 3×3cm/1×1in.
2. In a big pot, bring the water to a boil then add the meat, onion, half of the carrots, bay leaves and white peppercorns. Bring to the boil again, ladling off any froth. Cover, and boil the stew slowly for about 1½ hour. When 40 minutes remain, add the rest of the carrots.
3. Remove the meat from the liquid and place it into another pot, reserving 6 dl / 2 ½ cups of broth.
4. Melt the butter in the bottom of the pot and add the flour. Then add the broth. Bring to the boil, constantly stirring until it becomes a thick sauce. Return the meat to the pot and add the cream, lemon juice and sugar. Season with salt and pepper and add the dill. Goes well with freshly boiled potatoes.

SUPER PARTY CAKE

Makes 12–14 pieces:
Base:
250 g / ½ lb marzipan
125 g / ½ lb butter, room temperature
1 dl / ⅖ cup shredded coconut
3 eggs
1 dl / ⅖ cup plain flour

Rhubarb and white chocolate mousse:
200 g / ⅖ lb rhubarb
1 tbsp water
2 tbsp sugar
5 dl / 2 cups thick cream
200 g / ⅖ lb white chocolate
4 sheets of gelatine

Lemon curd with rhubarb:
300 g / ⅗ lb rhubarb, preferably pinkish red
½ dl / ¼ cup water
½ dl + 1 ½ dl / ⅕ + ⅔ cup sugar
2 eggs
2 tbsp lemon juice
2 sheets of gelatine
50 g / 2 oz butter

Garnish:
fresh strawberries

This recipe needs quite a lot of preparation, but when you see the delight on your guests' faces, you know it's been worth it. You can make the curd in advance to save time.

Here's how

1. Base: Preheat the oven to 175C/345F. Grate the marzipan and combine with the room-temperature butter. Mix in the coconut. Add the eggs one at the time and mix thoroughly. Sift in the flour.
2. Grease a springform pan 24cm/10in in diameter. Cover the bottom with the mix and bake in the middle of the oven for 25–30 minutes.

3. Mousse: Trim and cut the rhubarb into pieces. Boil with the sugar and a tbsp water. Cool and blend until smooth.
4. Whip the cream lightly. Melt the chocolate in a bowl over boiling water. Let it cool slightly before mixing it with the whipped cream. Stir until smooth.
5. Soak the gelatine sheets in cold water for about 5 minutes. Squeeze out the water. Melt with ½ dl / ¼ cup of the rhubarb purée in a small pot. Mix with the rest of the cooled purée. Fold in the chocolate cream using a rubber spatula.
6. Spread the mousse on top of the base and freeze for an hour. Then transfer to the fridge for at least 5 hours for the mousse to set.

7. Curd: Trim and cut the rhubarb into pieces. Boil the rhubarb, water and ½ dl / ¼ cup of sugar until mushy. Let cool. Blend into purée using a stick blender.
8. Beat the eggs with 1½ dl / ⅔ cup sugar in a pot. Add lemon juice and rhubarb purée. Place over a low heat and stir until you get a thick curd.
9. Soak the gelatine sheets in cold water for about 5 minutes. Squeeze out the water. Add to the hot curd and remove from heat. Now add the butter. Let it cool and keep in the fridge until serving.
10. Garnish the cake with strawberries and the rhubarb curd.

HARÖ

THE LAST FISHERMAN

Ten minutes northwest of Sandhamn are Harö island and the jetty at Hagede—the last port of call for the ferry after Sandhamn. To get there, we cross the bay of Rödkobbsfjärden and slip through the outer inlet.

Within seconds, the rough waves are gone and the water is calmer. Everything is still. We glide through the narrow passage and out into open water. On the port side we see the little inlet where Erik Lindström is waiting for us, feet planted solidly on the jetty. His cap is pulled down over his forehead, his grey moustache only just visible in the clear evening light. We're obviously being greeted by a real archipelago fisherman, old school.

Erik Lindström's jetty is built on an angle, and has space for a sizeable boathouse and several moorings. Today there are three boats of different sizes, among them Erik's fishing cutter and a smaller boat with an outboard engine.

This is where the islanders gather for occasional weddings and crayfish parties. The protected inlet is bathed in sunshine, and a black anchor glints on the sloping rock. The old bench, of the kind favoured for the telling of tall stories or for idle chat, is perfect for our conversation but it's obvious that Erik is unused to talking about himself. I have to draw him out.

Fishing was always Erik's passion from the day he left school on nearby island Djurö, aged only fifteen. He would get up at three o'clock in the morning, often making his way to the island's main fishing rocks at Horsten, where the red cabins are still in use.

But after years of commercial fishing, Erik had his sea change. He began cooking for paying customers. His boathouse attracted hungry visitors, from lunch guests to wedding parties. He could accommodate forty people at the most, smacking their lips over freshly fried perch fillets or his fillet of beef, always with a little shot of schnapps to accompany the starter.

"But it must be herb-infused," Erik insists.

On Harö, the houses are spread out and there is no longer a hub in the form of a hamlet. But several of the old buildings from the original Harö village are still there, around the bay that rising land has made almost unnavigable.

Erik Lindström and Moses the cat greet me at the jetty.

These days he sets out fishing nets only for his own needs, sometimes off his private jetty. But he still goes fishing almost every day, or at least three or four times a week.

There's a hint of pride in his voice when Erik mentions that he and his partner Anki are almost self-sustaining. They have one hundred and forty kilos of game in their freezer, and salad vegetables thrive in their greenhouse: tomatoes, cucumber and lettuce.

"I pat them a little every day," says Erik. "That way they grow nice and big—watering and fertilizing them isn't enough, you've got to talk to them too." Looking around, I see the large crates that Erik has made and filled with earth. The bright green leaves of new potatoes peeking over the sides of the crates reveal the treasures underneath.

When Erik was young, Harö was famous for its strawberry farms. Strawberries grew in every nook and cranny. The cows had to graze in the forests because the fields were taken over by strawberries. At the height of the island's success, five thousand punnets were being sent to Stockholm. Every single day.

But a shortage of labour, and, not least, the hard work involved, killed off the strawberry farms in the 1970s. Today most of the fields on Harö are overgrown, with aspen and brushwood replacing the rows of flowering plants.

Similarly, Erik changed lifestyle yet again. He currently makes his living as a carpenter in the winter and by doing odd-jobs for the council in the summer. Every once in a while he'll go over to Sandhamn for a cooking job and sometimes he'll get talked into serving dinner at the small island Horsten, perhaps serving his favourite pan-fried whitefish:

Gut and descale your whitefish and divide it so it will fit the frying pan. Fry in butter with the lid on, until it has some colour. Add thick cream to make a sauce and serve with new potatoes and a green salad.

But he still puzzles over how his mother prepared the pickled Baltic herring that she used to serve on crispbread.

"It doesn't matter how many times I try, I can never make it as good as hers."

Erik chuckles and strokes the cat lounging beside him on the sun-warmed rock, soft fur meeting a hand rough from hard work.

Inside Erik's boathouse, barrels of herring are fermenting in anticipation of traditional 'rotten herring' feasts at the end of summer.

Erik and I lay out fishing nets. Working boats used to be made of wood, now they're fibreglass or aluminium—and the sail has been replaced by the outboard motor.

Next page:
Decoys hanging on the boathouse wall. They fool seabirds into landing in the water close to the waiting hunter.

We lay out the net, Erik scarcely needing to check as he pays it out. I'm already imagining fish flapping in the net.

Back on Sandhamn, I sit down on the jetty with a cup of coffee. The sun is setting and in the distance I can see the silhouette of Harö's pine forest. I think about the old families who lived there. The people who farmed strawberries, caught their own fish and made a life in an environment so Spartan that it's hard to imagine. But they managed, one way or another.

Erik Lindström is one of the last true fishermen in the archipelago.

QUICK-CURED BLACKENED WHITEFISH

Serves 4:
400 g / 1 lb freshwater whitefish fillets, deboned
1 dl / ⅖ cup sugar
½ dl / ¼ cup salt
1 tsp crushed white peppercorns
2 tbsp finely chopped dill

We often fish for whitefish in summer. In this recipe, they should be cured for a few hours before being thrown on the barbecue. If you prefer it as a starter, lay the fillets on toasted sourdough bread (one per person) with a dab of horseradish cream.

Here's how

1. Combine the sugar, salt and white pepper.
2. Put the fillets in a plastic bag. Add the sugar-salt mix and the dill. Shake the bag and let the fish absorb the mix at room temperature for about 20 minutes to kick-start the curing process. Store in the fridge for another 2–3 hours.
3. Dry the fillets and put them in a barbecue fish basket. Cook the fish on the grill or over hot coals for 1–2 minutes on each side.

BALTIC HERRING FISH BALLS

Serves 4:
600 g / 1 ⅓ lb Baltic herring fillets
2 tbsp bread crumbs
½ dl / ¼ cup thick cream
1 egg
½ yellow onion
salt
freshly ground white pepper
butter to fry in

Baltic herring fish balls—could this be anything but Swedish? The oily herring meat is perfect for mincing and shaping into appetising small balls. Lingonberry preserve as an accompaniment is almost obligatory.

Here's how

1. Strip the skin off the herring. In a food processor, blend the fish to a paste.
2. Combine breadcrumbs and cream in a bowl and let swell for a while.
3. Mix the fish paste with the breadcrumbs and cream then add the egg. Grate the onion and add to the mix. Season with salt and pepper.
4. Roll into small balls. Fry in butter evenly about 8–10 minutes.

Tip

Clean the herring by cutting off the head and tail fin then open along the backbone to cut out the fillets.

FISH STEW, HARÖ-STYLE

Serves 4:
600 g / 1 ⅓ lb cod fillets
2 dl / ⅘ cup white wine
5 dl / 2 cups water
1 fish stock cube
½ tsp lemon pepper seasoning
2 carrots
1 leek
1 fennel bulb
1 parsnip
150 g / ⅓ lb green asparagus
8 cherry tomatoes
small packet of saffron (0.5g)
300 g / ⅔ lb cooked and peeled fresh shrimp
2 tbsp chopped chives
salt
freshly ground black pepper

Several mild flavours contribute character to this delicate stew using white wine and saffron. Bake a loaf of French bread to make it more fancy. Or spread garlic butter on thin slices of store-bought French bread and put them under the oven grill for about 10 minutes at 200C/390F. For added taste, mix in a dollop of aioli at the end.

Here's how

1. Cut the cod into small chunks. Salt the fish about an hour before cooking.
2. Bring wine, water, stock cube and lemon pepper to the boil.
3. Cut the carrots into "coins", the leek and fennel into strips, the parsnip into cubes and the asparagus into small sticks.
4. Add all the vegetables to the boiling liquid. Add the saffron and cook all the vegetables until almost done (al dente).
5. Drain the fish in a colander. Poach in the stew for 5 minutes.
6. Top with the shrimps and chives. Season with salt and pepper.

MOOSE BURGERS

Serves 4:
1 dl / ⅖ cup thick cream
1 tsp potato starch
1 tbsp breadcrumbs
500 g / 1 ¼ lb minced moose meat
1 tbsp finely chopped onion
1 egg yolk
3 tbsp grated mature cheese, e.g. Västerbotten or Präst
1 tsp salt
a generous pinch of freshly ground black pepper
butter to fry in

Moose mince is fantastic for hamburgers and meatballs. My sons wolf this down. The meat has a strong flavour of venison and can be complemented with lingonberry preserve and potatoes. If you can't find moose mince, substitute mince fom other game meat or venison.

Here's how

1. Combine the cream, potato starch and breadcrumbs in a bowl and let swell for 5 minutes.
2. Add the minced meat, onion, egg yolk and cheese and mix until smooth. Season with salt and pepper.
3. Shape the mince into 8 burgers. Fry in butter for about 5 minutes on each side. Serve with mashed potatoes, lingonberry preserve and steamed sugar snaps.

HERRING: PICKLED, AND ARCHIPELAGO STYLE

PICKLED
Makes 4–6 portions:
6 salted herring fillets soaked in water for 8 hours
1 dl / ⅖ cup spirit vinegar, 12%
2 dl / ⅘ cup sugar
3 dl / 1 ¼ cups water
½ tsp salt
1 red onion
2 bunches of fresh summer carrots
10 allspice berries
1 tsp mustard seeds
3 bay leaves
a bunch of fresh dill

ARCHIPELAGO STYLE
Makes 4–6 portions:
400 g / 1 lb matjes herring or soused herring
1 ½ dl / ⅔ cup sour cream
2 tbsp mayonnaise, preferably homemade
4 tbsp whitefish caviar or lumpfish caviar
2 tbsp finely chopped chives

Every time we have herring I wonder why we don't do it more often, whether it's served as the main dish for an outdoor lunch, or as a starter. When you take that first mouthful, with a side of new potatoes, your mouth automatically smiles.

Here's how
Pickled:
1. Bring the vinegar, sugar and water to a boil. Remove from the heat and let cool.
2. Peel and slice the onion and carrots. Layer in a glass jar with allspice, mustard seeds, bay leaves and dill. Pour over the pickling vinegar.
3. Let the herring set and infuse in the fridge for a minimum of 24 hours before serving.

Archipelago style:
1. Drain the matjes herring. Combine sour cream, mayonnaise, caviar and chives in a bowl. Add the herring and pour everything into a glass jar.
2. Let the herring set in the fridge for a minimum of 3 hours before serving.

MELON DESSERT

Serves 4–6:
1 cantaloupe or honeydew melon (approx. 600 g / 1 ⅓ lb)
2 tbsp water
6 tbsp sugar
1 ½ tsp mint leaves cut into thin slivers
blackcurrant sorbet
a little dessert wine, optional

Several people in our family are either lactose-intolerant or allergic to milk protein. So this dessert is ideal, since it contains no dairy products.

And it has a really fresh taste. The best accompaniment is a currant sorbet but any tart sorbet such as raspberry or lemon will do.

Here's how

1. Boil the sugar and water for a few minutes. Set aside and let cool while you peel and dice the melon.
2. Mix the melon and mint with the syrup. Serve slightly warm with the sorbet. If you like, drizzle with dessert wine (a nice Sauternes?) before serving.

GRÖNSKÄR

A LIGHTHOUSE KEEPER FOR A NEW ERA

Over the years I have often stood on the shore at Sandhamn, gazing at the Grönskär lighthouse. You can see the old 18th-century construction rising up on the horizon. The island itself is so small you almost wouldn't notice it. It's as if the island doesn't want to upstage the lighthouse known as the Queen of the Baltic, built using only a water-colour as the architect's drawing.

The Grönskär lighthouse was meant to be built in sandstone from Gotland but there was not enough to complete the building. So granite was hewn from the local rocks, giving the lighthouse its slightly mottled appearance.

There's something monumental about the mottled stone edifice, something that reminds me of old-time lighthouse keepers. Of single rays of light cutting through the fog. Of lost sailing ships searching for a harbour. Lighthouse keeping is a lonely existence, hard to imagine, and yet the lighthouse itself is a vital symbol for sailors returning from long voyages. A landmark, showing the way to safety.

As we approach Grönskär, I see a handful of houses and simple cabins, all clinging to the rocks. The mouth of the old harbour has silted up, making it scarcely navigable. I've scraped my propeller here more than once, so we decide to use the southern harbour today. It's shallow too, and I have to lean over the bow to check for underwater rocks.

We tie up and use the wooden walkways to find our way to Fredrik Sjöblom, one of the founders of the tourism/adventure company Sandhamn Guides. He is currently renting the old lighthouse keeper's residence, which is owned by the Archipelago Foundation, whose mission is to protect the archipelago and at the same time make it more accessible to the public.

Fredrik, who grew up on Sandhamn, has just finished mowing the little lawn in front of his lodgings.

The neat lawn emphasises the harshness of the surroundings—the rough rocks, the crevices in the cliffs. Not far off, cow parsley and buttercups growing in a tiny summer meadow add to the contrasts.

All kinds of people come here, from company executives to construction teams. Anyone who is seeking inner peace. Fredrik points out the

flat, sloping rocks worn smooth by the water over the centuries, and the waves rolling in.

I realise that there is little to do here except enjoy nature. Perhaps meditate on the sea swells, or just make the most of a picnic basket?

"Even people with serious stress-related problems can unwind out here," says Fredrik, winking, and adds: "Somehow it's easier to breathe on Grönskär."

Fredrik shows us around the lighthouse keeper's rooms, where multi-occupancy bedrooms, in muted colours, await overnight guests. The ceilings were repainted only two years ago but need another coat—a reminder of the ever-present damp, and of the fact that buildings in the outer skerries need constant maintenance.

Meals are served on a long wooden table outside. Everything is cooked and prepared on Sandhamn. It's often grilled fish; pike-perch and cod are Fredrik's favourites.

What's the best flavouring? "Horseradish," he declares. "But it has to be fresh so there's a kick to it."

"This is where I had my wedding dinner," he says, running his hand over the worn surface of the table. His expression softens and he fingers his wedding ring.

"It was the summer of 2011. Tove and I were married on the south beach at Sandhamn and took the boat out here." He pauses. "It just felt natural to come to Grönskär."

We walk over to the lighthouse and climb the tower. There are eighty-four steps—I counted. And they're higher than normal steps so you have to lift up your feet, which means you're tired by the end. From the top level, a narrow ladder in white cast-iron leads up to the lantern itself. There's room for only a few people at a time. But, oh! The view!

In front of us are hundreds—no, thousands—of skerries and rocks. The islands have jagged edges and the sea is completely flat. I begin to question whether Galileo could have been wrong; perhaps the earth isn't round at all? In the distance the Almagrundet lighthouse can be

From the lantern at the top you can see for miles. Fredrik points out the Almagrundet lighthouse visible on the horizon.

From the air, Grönskär's exposed position is clear. It's easy to imagine winter waves crashing over the island.

glimpsed. It's all so beautiful I can't help but wonder if God doesn't abide somewhere out there where the sun is sparkling.

Later, we walk all around Grönskär island, over bare reefs and crevices so packed with juniper bushes that you can't find a foothold. We have to be careful; adders are common, even though the island is small.

We chat about earning a living out in the archipelago and how Fredrik and his partner started Sandhamn Guides at the end of the 1990s.

"I wanted to stay out here," he says reflectively. "Running some kind of business ... that connected with nature. What we have here is unique."

Conversation turns to the problems families have in the outer skerries, like having school-age children on an island with no school. These days, the family lives on the mainland during the week, but Fredrik's registered address is on Sandhamn. It works, but it's not easy, despite modern communications. Fredrik shrugs.

"When has life in the archipelago ever been easy?"

It's time to leave. Just as we manoeuvre cautiously out of the narrow bay, the sun comes out. It strikes the top of the lighthouse, as though someone had switched on the electricity to say goodbye.

Fredrik is standing up on the rocks, arms folded. I can still hear the fervour in his words: "I'll never leave the archipelago."

A new kind of lighthouse keeper.

This old coffee pot has been in use on Grönskär for over fifty years.

The new generation of archipelago residents are entrepreneurs. Fredrik leads a kayak safari from its starting point on Grönskär.

Next page: The lighthouse, popularly known as the Queen of the Baltic.

PICNIC WRAPS

Serves 4 people:
2 chicken breasts
1 ½ tbsp olive oil
salt
freshly ground black pepper
4 flour tortillas, medium size
8 leaves of Romaine lettuce
6 tbsp sweet chili sauce
100 g / ¼ lb sliced or grated Västerbotten or Parmesan cheese

Wraps are perfect for picnics because it's so simple to roll up everything in a tortilla then package it in plastic film or a sheet of baking paper. For me, Swedish Västerbotten cheese is in the same class as Parmesan cheese —here it's in a combo with sweet chili sauce. You'll love it, I promise.

Here's how

1. Cut the chicken into small pieces and fry in oil until golden brown. Season with salt and pepper.
2. Lay a lettuce leaves flat on a tortilla. Spoon over the sweet chili and chicken while it's still hot. Quickly spread the cheese on top so it starts to melt.
3. Fold nice and tight and wrap in clingfilm or baking paper to keep them soft.

CINNAMON BUNS

Makes about 30 buns:
Dough:
100 g / ¼ lb butter
5 dl / 2 ⅕ cups whole milk
50 g / 2 oz fresh yeast or
5 tsp active dried yeast
½ tsp salt
½ dl / ¼ cup sugar
2 tsp coarsely crushed black
cardamom seeds
13–15 dl / 5 ½ – 6 ⅓ cups
plain flour
(800–900 g / 1 ¾ – 2 lb)

Filling and topping:
200 g / ½ lb butter, room
temperature
2 dl / ⅘ cup sugar
2 tbsp ground cinnamon
2 eggs for glazing
1 dl / ⅖ cup nib sugar

Nothing pleases my eldest son more than when I bake cinnamon buns. Big, round, fat buns stuffed with filling! He can't get enough of them! You can vary the filling, but cardamom is a great substitute for the cinnamon.

Here's how

1. Melt the butter in a pot and add the milk. Heat to about 37C/98F.
2. Crumble the yeast into a bowl and pour over the heated milk. Stir to dissolve the yeast. Add salt, sugar and cardamom.
3. Slowly add the flour and work into a smooth dough. Save 1 dl / ⅖ cup flour for later. Let the dough rise under a tea towel for about an hour.
4. Roll the dough flat and spread the butter on top. Sprinkle sugar evenly over the butter and dust with cinnamon. Roll the dough into a snake and cut into approximately 30 slices. Place the slices flat on a baking tray lined with baking paper. Cover with a tea towel and let rise another 30 minutes. Heat the oven to 225C/435F.
5. Brush the buns with the egg wash and sprinkle with nib sugar. Bake in the middle of the oven for about 10 minutes.

RHUBARB WRAPS

Makes 6 small wraps:
4 rhubarb stalks (approx. 400 g / 1 lb)
3 tbsp butter
1 dl / ⅖ cup cane sugar
1 tsp cinnamon
1 ½ dl / ⅔ cup walnuts
100 g / ¼ lb marzipan
6 small size flour tortillas
vanilla ice cream
sugar and cinnamon to sprinkle on top

It's fun to invent different things to do with rhubarb when the kitchen garden is awash with their purple leaves. These sweet & sour wraps work best slightly warm and with a scoop of vanilla ice cream, but when you're out in the skerries, they're just as good cold.

Here's how

1. Trim and cut the rhubarb into small pieces. Melt the butter in a frying pan and add the rhubarb, sugar, cinnamon and roughly chopped walnuts.
2. Braise the rhubarb until it softens and mix in the grated marzipan. Let cool.
3. Divide the filling between the tortillas and fold into wraps. Fry the wraps in butter until golden brown. Sprinkle with sugar and cinnamon.
4. Serve with vanilla ice cream.

SAUSAGE WITH POTATO SALAD

Serves 4:
500 g / 1 ¼ lb new potatoes
4 bunches of fresh Summer carrots
250 g / ½ lb green asparagus
1 red onion
3 tbsp olive oil
1 ½ tbsp white wine vinegar
1 tbsp whole-grain mustard
½ tbsp honey
1 bunch of radishes
salt
freshly ground black pepper
2 tbsp finely chopped chives
400 g / 1 lb sausage, e.g. kabanos or chorizo

A fancy potato salad with carrots, asparagus and radishes. It's easy to throw together (even for a crowd) and easy to carry on a picnic. Barbecue the sausages on the spot. Try a spicy kind!

Here's how

1. Scrub the potatoes and carrots. Cut the carrots into pieces. Break off the tough ends of the asparagus and discard.
2. Boil the potatoes in salted water for roughly 20 minutes. After about 10 minutes, add the carrots. Add the asparagus about 3 minutes before the potatoes are done. Drain the vegetables. Leave the steaming potatoes and carrots drying in a colander and put the asparagus in a bowl of ice-cold water.
3. Peel and slice the onion thin. Combine oil, vinegar, mustard and honey in a large bowl.
4. Trim and cut the radishes in half. Cut the potatoes into small chunks and cut the asparagus lengthwise. Stir the potatoes, carrots, asparagus and radishes with the dressing. Season with salt and pepper. Mix in the chives.
5. Serve with grilled spicy sausages.

SMOKED FISH PICNIC SANDWICH

Makes 4 sandwiches:
½ dl / ¼ cup spirit vinegar (12%)
1 dl / ⅖ cup sugar
1 ½ dl / ⅔ cup water
½ tsp salt
½ cucumber
½ bunch of radishes
1 baguette
½ dl / ¼ cup cream cheese
1 tbsp freshly grated horse-radish
400 g / 1 lb smoked fish (whitefish, kippers or mackerel)
1 punnet garden cress
flaked sea salt
freshly ground black pepper

It's easy to take the ham-and-cheese route when planning sandwiches for an outing. Here's an alternative with the lovely zing of horseradish. A few minutes in spirit vinegar make cucumber and radishes extra tasty.

Here's how

1. Combine vinegar, sugar, water and salt in a bowl. Stir until it dissolves.
2. Slice the cucumber and radishes and add to the liquor. Let marinate for at least 10 minutes.
3. Spread the cream cheese on to the baguette and add grated horseradish, fish, cress and the pickled vegetables.
4. Toss some flaked sea salt and black pepper on top. Serve immediately or wrap them for a picnic.

BREAD ON A STICK WITH GUBBRÖRA

Serves 4:
4 eggs
4 anchovy fillets or herring (alternatively, Matjes herring)
4 tbsp mayonnaise, preferably homemade
1 tbsp Swedish cod roe spread (optional)
1 tbsp finely chopped chives
salt
freshly ground black pepper

Makes 8 sticks:
4 dl / 1 ¾ cups plain flour
½ tsp flaked sea salt
2 tsp baking powder
a large pinch of aniseed
50 g / 1 ¾ oz butter
1 ½ dl / ⅔ cup sour cream

Bread on a stick and gubbröra *(roughly: "bloke's mix", once a staple at working men's cafés) is a great and unexpected combo. Pre-mix all the dry ingredients at home in the kitchen and it's easy to punch it into a dough with butter and sour cream just before cooking over hot coals. Hot bread on an archipelago skerry—life doesn't get any better!*

Here's how
Gubbröra:
1. Hard-boil the eggs. Cool, peel and roughly chop them.
2. Chop the fish finely. Mix with mayonnaise, chives and cod roe. Season with salt and pepper.

Bread on a stick:
1. Combine all the dry ingredients in a bowl (or a plastic bag).
2. Cut the butter into the flour and squeeze between fingers and thumbs until you get it to the size of small peas. Add the sour cream and quickly work into a smooth dough.
3. Divide the dough into 8 pieces. Roll into long sausages and twist them around sticks. Grill over coals on all sides for about 8–10 minutes.

LYGNA

LIVING ON THE EDGE

Sky and sea fuse as we approach Lygna, four nautical miles north of the Svenska Högarna group.

Bare rocks protrude from the water, as though a giant hand had thrust them up from the sea floor without a second thought. The island is almost without vegetation—only a few gnarled trees and yellow moss in irregular patterns on the rocks. The waters are dotted with shallows.

There! The inlet, hidden behind cliffs, is so narrow and concealed that we almost miss it. It looks as if somebody hacked it out on a whim. But once inside, it's flat and calm, unbelievably still after the rough seas we've just crossed.

We're on Hamnskär, the main island, where Magdalena Rinaldo and her husband Sten keep a protective eye on Lygna's bird population, just as Magdalena's father once did. Sten Rinaldo, who wrote books about the archipelago, spent many years on the Lygna islands.

A long, narrow jetty creeps along the steep cliff-face, and opposite we spy a few wind-blown cabins. They have been there since the 1700s and are equipped in the old style—two beds, a kitchenette and a tiny storage closet.

Magdalena greets me on the jetty dressed in a pretty, flowered summer dress. "You're here already?" she says, chiding me. "I haven't had time to get ready."

Behind her, Frida, a brown and white spaniel, is wagging her tail. Tarzan, the biggest cat I've ever seen, comes padding along behind.

Magdalena keeps a close eye on him—last summer, a hungry sea eagle dived at Tarzan, talons at the ready, and only a metre before bird met cat, a screaming and gesticulating Magdalena scared the bird off. She has not let the cat out of her sight since.

Once the boat has been tied up, Magdalena shows us her tiny kitchen. A kerosene lamp hangs on the wall as the sole light source. The kitchen reminds me of a boat's galley, but is actually a wall incorporating a work surface, shelves and an oven, with several cleverly placed hooks.

Magdalena Rinaldo has picked a bunch of meadowsweet for me to take home.

Magdalena and her husband Sten live in this tiny hut on Hamnskär for half the year.

The oven has only one setting—low/medium—and only two hotplates, but has produced a multitude of delicious meals!

"It's an adventure, cooking with such limited means," says Magdalena. "It's my thing. I can poach flounder fillets in wine, for example. Or Julia's flounder, the way all kids like it, even the ones who say they don't like fish."

Sometimes the menu includes kelp potatoes, which involves putting a little water in the pot then filling it with well-rinsed kelp. Magdalena boils the potatoes in advance when she needs the hotplates for other things, then wraps the pot in a blanket and tucks it up in bed to keep warm, checking constantly that Frida or Tarzan don't lie on it. Or her husband!

Desserts are not the norm on Lygna. Available ingredients are limited to cloudberries and blackcurrants, plus wild raspberries of course. Mostly, dessert is berries with sugar and cream, sometimes eaten with the fingers. And raspberry pudding if it's a feast!

Lygna has no electricity, no running water and no refrigeration. So Magdalena has a homemade cooler: an old firewood crate in one of the huts. She fills it with coarse salt to a depth of about 25cm/10in. Butter, milk cartons and cheese sit on top of the salt, and to my astonishment remain refrigerator-cool. I touch the cold surface and wonder out loud: "How can this be possible?"

Magdalena grins broadly—I'm not the first to react like that.

Behind the house, a natural hollow in the cliff was once a rainwater reservoir. It was kept scrubbed scrupulously clean so the water would be safe to drink. Now the bottom is covered in algae and the water is stagnant and brackish. But the reservoir is an indication of human inventiveness, finding solutions against all odds.

Close by is Magdalena's kitchen garden, tucked away in rock crevices with just enough soil to allow things to grow. I spot garden beds smaller than half a square metre. Magdalena points out the leeks sticking up beside the parsley. The purple tops of chives wave in the breeze. With a

Magdalena's cottage just has room for two beds with a table in between. The ceiling height makes standing uncomfortable for those who aren't short of stature.

Magdalena has collected her best recipes in a notebook that she has illustrated with cute drawings.

Next page: The ingenious kitchen is really only a wall with kitchen equipment, but has everything you need for cooking excellent food.

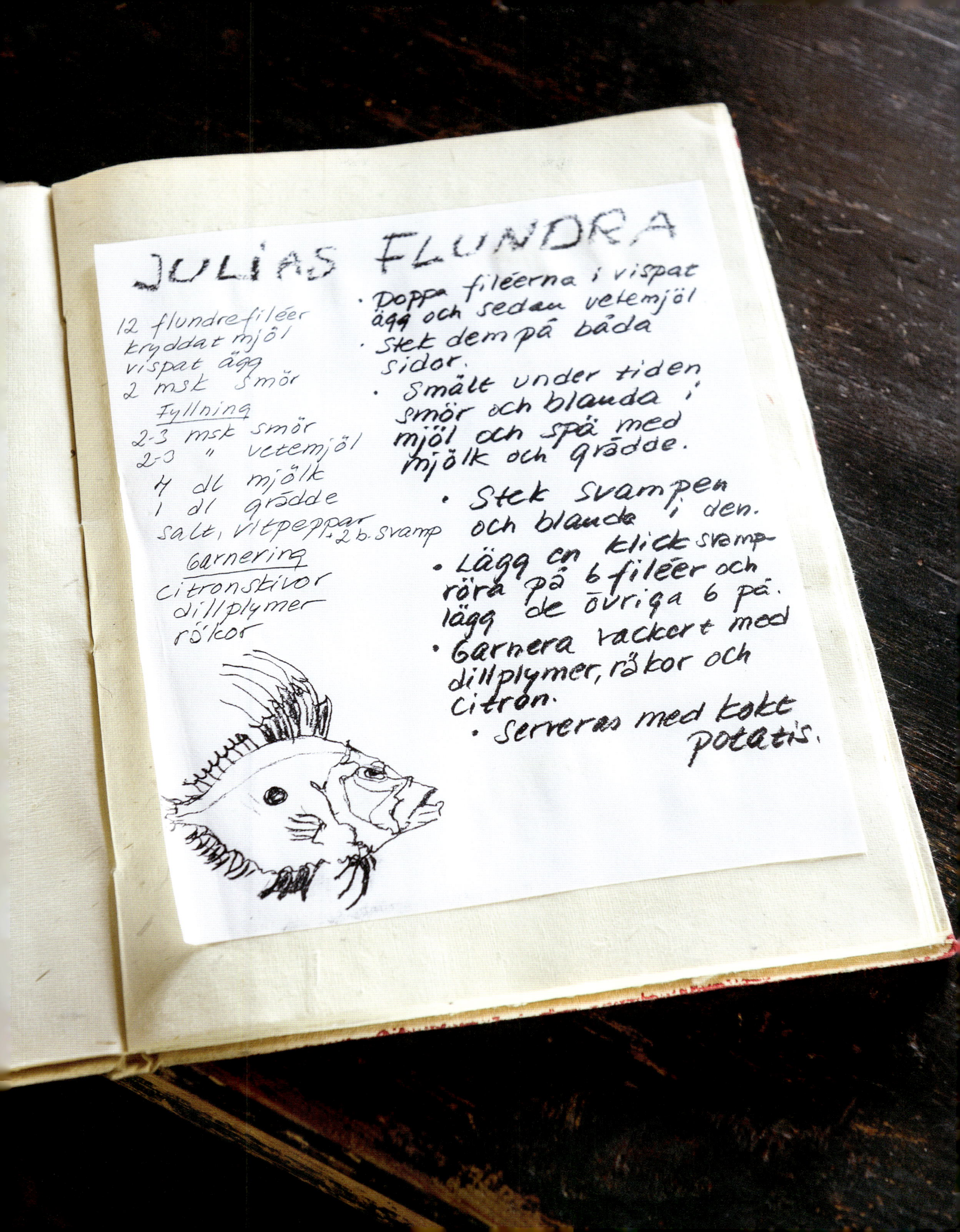

JULIAS FLUNDRA

12 flundrefiléer
kryddat mjöl
vispat ägg
2 msk smör

Fyllning

2-3 msk smör
2-3 " vetemjöl
4 dl mjölk
1 dl grädde
salt, vitpeppar + 2 b. svamp

Garnering

citronskivor
dillplymer
räkor

- Doppa filéerna i vispat ägg och sedan vetemjöl
- Stek dem på båda sidor.
- Smält under tiden smör och blanda i mjöl och spä med mjölk och grädde.
- Stek svampen och blanda i den.
- Lägg en klick svamp-röra på 6 filéer och lägg de övriga 6 på.
- Garnera vackert med dillplymer, räkor och citron.
- Serveras med kokt potatis.

DROSTE'S
CACAO
OCEAN QUEEN
COFFEE

wink, she takes my hand and leads me to a sunny nook protected from wind and rain.

Standing in a rectangular bed built from and bordered by granite stones, the soil covered by kelp, is a neat line of grapevines. The vines are held proudly erect by bamboo canes, and with their pale green leaves they could easily come from a French *vallée*.

I gape, and Magdalena laughs.

"We don't get many grapes, but even a few isn't bad," she says with satisfaction. "We grow things in crevices wherever we can. That's the way they used to do it here in the outer skerries."

Magdalena worries about the archipelago.

"It's too quiet," she says. "No eiders quacking, no scoters squawking. There are hardly any seabirds left out here."

Ten years ago she could count eider nests by the thousand, but now it's by the dozen. She sighs.

"When you're tracing your own footsteps year after year, you notice the differences, however small."

Magdalena disappears behind a cliff and returns with a bunch of meadowsweet. She tells me to crush the bud, and it gives off a strong scent of something familiar that I just can't place.

She nods. "It contains acetylsalicylic acid. You can also use willow bark to bring down a fever. And it makes delicious tea as well."

I'm holding an ancient substitute for aspirin in my hand. It's news to me, but useful knowledge.

It's time to leave. Before I do, I am given a peppermint cutting to plant on Sandhamn. A souvenir from Lygna. As I leave the sheltered bay, a small flock of seabirds bobbing on the waves makes way for us. And, yes, I hear eiders quacking.

Tarzan is the real king of Lygna. He's the biggest cat I have ever seen.

The pantry is like the kitchen—minimal but functional, with eggs and vegetables in small baskets and drying herbs hanging from the ceiling.

Next page: From the air it's clear that Lygna has a great harbour. A protected mooring place is essential for living in the outer skerries.

JULIA'S FLOUNDER

Serves 4:
10 flounder fillets (or other fillet of white fish, e.g. perch or cod)
2 dl / ⅘ cup plain flour
salt
freshly ground black pepper
2 eggs
butter

Creamed mushrooms:
300 g mushrooms (e.g. chanterelles or button mushrooms)
3 tbsp butter
1 tbsp plain flour
2 dl / ⅘ cup milk
1 dl / ⅖ cup thick cream
salt
freshly ground black pepper

Garnish:
400 g / 1 lb peeled cooked shrimp
2 tbsp finely chopped chives or dill
2 lemons

To serve:
freshly boiled potatoes tossed in butter, dill

"I don't know how many children who said they didn't like fish changed their minds after eating this," says Magdalena Rinaldo with a grin. For her youngest daughter, Julia, it's a birthday treat.

Here's how

1. Boil the potatoes in salted water.
2. Creamed mushrooms: Sauté the mushrooms in butter. Sift the flour over the mushrooms and continue to sauté. Add the milk and cream and boil over low heat until creamy and smooth. Season with salt and pepper.
3. Coating: Combine flour, salt and white pepper on a plate. Beat the eggs in a bowl. Dip the fillets in the seasoned flour first, then in the egg. Fry them in butter for about 3 minutes on each side.
4. Fry the boiled potatoes in butter for about 5 minutes and then add some dill.
5. Top the fish with creamed mushrooms and shrimps. Toss over the finely chopped chives or dill. Serve with the dill potatoes and a lemon wedge.

SMOKED SALMON WITH MUSTARD SAUCE

Serves 4:
400 g / 1 lb cold smoked salmon, sliced thin
2 tbsp finely chopped chives

extras:
3 tbsp capers
lemon wedges

Sauce:
1 tsp soaked and crushed mustard seeds
2 tbsp sweet mustard
2 tbsp brown sugar
1 tbsp HP sauce
1 tbsp Japanese soy sauce
1 tbsp Worcestershire sauce
1 tbsp balsamic vinegar
1 tbsp finely chopped dill
2 tbsp olive oil

This works well as one of several small dishes for a buffet. Otherwise, the recipe should be enough for a main course for four. Don't worry if you don't have all the sauce ingredients—you can leave out one or two, promises Magdalena.

Here's how

1. Start with the sauce: Soak the mustard seeds for an hour or so. Crush them coarsely using a mortar and pestle. Mix all the ingredients except the oil, which you add a drop at a time.
2. Lay the salmon on a platter and drizzle some oil on top. Toss the chives (and optionally, capers) over the salmon. Serve with lemon wedges.

LYGNA'S ARCHIPELAGO STEW

Serves 4:
800 g / 1 ¾ lb perch fillet or similar fish with white flesh, preferably not whitefish
6 carrots
8 tomatoes
100 g / ¼ lb butter
2 tbsp finely chopped dill
3 dl / 1 ¼ cups fish stock (not from concentrate)
salt
freshly ground black pepper

What a treat! This dish must be poached in butter, with no water. Take the pot off the heat a few minutes before the fish is done and let it finish in the hot sauce. Mashed or boiled potatoes are a good side dish.

Here's how

1. Peel the carrots and blanch them in lightly salted water. Slice the tomatoes.
2. Fillet the fish. If using perch, cut a narrow V into the fillet from the head side to get rid of the extra row of bones. Lightly season with salt and pepper.
3. Melt half the butter in a pot. Cover the bottom of the pot with tomatoes. In layers, add the fish, carrots, dill and dabs of butter. Lightly season each layer with salt. Cover the final layer with thin slices of butter and chopped dill. Pour the fish stock over.
4. Carefully boil over low heat until the fish is cooked. Perch and flounder will cook fast: 5–10 minutes. Cod will take a little longer. Season with salt and pepper.

MARINATED, SMOKED WHITEFISH

Serves 4:
smoked whitefish,
approx. 800 g / 1 ¾ lb

Marinade:
2 dl / ⁴⁄₅ cup olive oil
½ dl / ¼ cup vinegar or
lemon juice
2 dl / ⁴⁄₅ cup white wine
1 ½ tbsp mustard
½ leek, sliced thinly
salt
freshly ground black pepper

Potato salad:
600 g / 1 ⅓ lb new potatoes
2 dl / ⁴⁄₅ cup white wine
2 tbsp apple cider vinegar
1 tsp French mustard
2 tbsp olive oil
2 tbsp water
½ tsp herb salt
1 red onion, finely chopped
½ leek, sliced finely
2 tbsp chives, finely
chopped
3 tbsp capers

It's best to use flat-smoked whitefish—fish detached from the spine and spread so it is smoked through, and not left raw by the spinal bone.

The marinade is based on writer Izaak Walton's 17th-century recipe from his 1653 book The Compleat Angler, *still widely read and available in a new edition.*

Here's how

1. Mix the marinade and pour it over the fish. Let it absorb for at least 4 hours, preferably overnight.
2. Boil the potatoes in salted water. Cut into halves and transfer to a bowl while still warm.
3. Pour over the wine and let it rest for 10 minutes. Combine the rest of the ingredients to make the sauce. Drain the potatoes from the wine and mix them with the sauce. Garnish with chives and capers.

Remember

The fish should marinate for at least four hours to absorb all the flavours. Ideally, overnight.

FLOUNDER-SCHNITZEL

Serves 4:
10 fillets (600–800 g / 1 ⅓–1 ¾ lb) flounder, fresh or frozen (any other white fish will do fine)
salt
freshly ground black pepper
1 tbsp butter
1 egg
1 dl / ⅖ cup bread crumbs
½ dl / ¼ cup finely grated cheese, e.g. Parmesan or Västerbotten cheese
1 tsp salt
1 tsp cayenne pepper

Garnish:
1 lemon
approx. 55 g / 2 oz anchovy fillets (1 can Swedish sprats)
approx. 350 g / ¾ lb green olives

Use any flat fish, fresh or frozen. Just remember to trim off the white skin on the stomach, it can taste like blubber. The coating of Parmesan or Västerbotten cheese likens this dish with a classic wienerschnitzel. Good ideas are meant to varied upon, like with this flounder.

Here's how

1. Rub the fillets with salt and pepper.
2. Melt the butter on low heat, beat the egg and mix. Brush the mix on the fillets.
3. Combine the breadcrumbs, grated cheese, salt and cayenne pepper. Coat the fillets with the breadcrumb mix.
4. Fry the fish golden brown in butter, about 2 minutes on each side.
5. Garnish each fish with a thin slice of lemon and an anchovy fillet rolled around an olive.
6. Serve the fish with a crispy green salad and freshly boiled kelp potatoes (see page 114).

COD À LA MEDITERRANEAN

Serves 4:
800 g / 1 ¾ lb white fish (cod or flatfish)
3 tbsp butter
2–3 cloves of garlic
1 orange, grated zest and freshly squeezed juice
3 dl / 1 ¼ cup torn white bread (easiest with stale bread)
1 dl / ⅖ cup finely chopped flat leaved parsley
salt
freshly ground black pepper

When you want to go crazy with garlic, this is a great way, with the crispy, spicy coating and its orange and parsley flavours. If you're counting calories, use less butter and more orange juice.

Here's how

1. Preheat the oven to 200C/390F. Season the fish with salt and pepper and place in a ovenproof dish.
2. Melt the butter in a frying pan. Add crushed garlic, grated zest and juice from the orange. Make sure to scrub the orange first and use only the orange part of the peel.
3. Toss in the bread and parsley. Let it sauté slightly. If it looks too dry, add more butter.
4. Spread the mix on top of the fish and cook in the middle of the oven for 20 minutes.
5. Serve with potatoes tossed in butter (see page 122) and a fresh green salad.

RASPBERRY DESSERT

Serves 4:
225 g / ½ lb raspberries, fresh or frozen (thawed)
1 ½ tbsp potato starch
1 + ½ dl / ⅖ + ¼ cup sugar + 6 tbsp for the moulds
2 egg whites
2 egg yolks
butter
icing sugar

Yummy! Raspberry pudding for dessert! So smooth it melts on your tongue!

All you need is a punnet of raspberries and a couple of eggs.

Okay, maybe a few other ingredients and a little electric whisk. And a couple of crunchy oat crisps wouldn't hurt.

Here's how

1. In a pot, whip up raspberries, potato starch and 1 dl / ½ cup of sugar. Bring to a boil over low heat and cook until you get a smooth custard. Let it cool at room temperature.
2. Set the oven for 200C/390F. Carefully grease the moulds and dust with sugar.
3. Beat the egg whites frothy using an electric whisk. Add ½ dl / ¼ cup sugar (a little at the time) and beat to a stiff meringue.
4. Beat the egg yolks with the raspberry custard. Fold in the meringue with a rubber spatula.
5. Fill the moulds to the brim and flatten the top using a spatula or a butter knife. With a finger, loosen the pudding along the top of the rim so the batter can rise while baking.
6. Bake in the middle of the oven for 12–15 minutes. The pudding should still be a little creamy in the centre. Dust with icing sugar and serve immediately.

SVENSKA HÖGARNA

SARAH OF THE OUTPOST

Landing on Svenska Högarna I find I'm much too close to a bird's nest. Two angry arctic terns appear from nowhere, one repeatedly attempting to peck at my head. It's like a scene from the Hitchcock film *The Birds*. The irate parents literally chase me off. From a safe distance, Sarah Anderin laughs at the spectacle.

Sarah must be one of the happiest lighthouse keepers in Sweden, a positive dynamo who has settled on the Svenska Högarna nature reserve, eighty kilometres from Stockholm at the outer extremity of the archipelago. Off the islands is a long row of reefs notorious as one of the world's largest maritime graveyards.

This is where Sarah lives with husband Alf, their three children, and Sarah's in-laws—seven in all, three generations, living year-round on one of Sweden's most isolated islands.

For example, in the winter of 2012/13, it took months before the mainland could be reached by other means than helicopter. Ridges of sea ice made it impossible to leave the island, either by boat or snowmobile.

Svenska Högarna has been a weather station continuously since 1874. "The weather's always on my mind," says Sarah. It is a vital part of life at a coastal and weather station, all the more so when it's the last outpost before the Baltic Sea.

But for Sarah, food rather than weather is the focus.

"I just love cooking!" she exclaims as she sets the table with buns and coffee in her snug kitchen.

Svenska Högarna may be isolated, but the red wooden turn of the century house boasts both a refrigerator and a freezer, running water, plus electricity from the island's small, diesel-driven generator.

Fish is obviously a mainstay of the family's diet, along with anything else that nature provides, such as potatoes from their own patch, herb butter made with home-grown herbs, and fresh onions. Summer brings cloudberries and currants, enough to fill large baskets. Cherries

The Baltic Sea extends outside the window of the red wooden cottage. When the sea is as flat and calm as this, it's hard to imagine that the reefs off the island are one of the world's largest maritime graveyards, where hundreds of ships have come to grief.

Sarah on her stairs scrubbing potatoes in the afternoon sun. On the menu tonight is blackened salmon and potatoes with horseradish. Many varieties of herbs are growing in the pots.

An angry arctic tern swooped at me when I tied up the boat too close to her nest.

Next page: The cemetery on Svenska Högarna looks more like a summer meadow, with its cow parsley and a sea of midsummer blooms. In the background, the well-known lighthouse beacon, built in 1874.

are another favourite, as are blueberries, but both have to be imported from the mainland. It's worth it for a dessert of stewed cherries with creamy ice cream. Yum!

And then there's the coffee break.

Sarah loves coffee breaks (*fika* in Swedish), especially at weekends. Family *fika* has become a summer tradition for the Anderins. There'll be home-baked buns, cookies, cakes and Sarah's iced tea à la maison for the adults.

Sarah breaks off:

"I'm beginning to sound like a fanatic foodie—but we don't make everything from scratch. Sometimes we're in a hurry." With a smile she opens the fridge and indicates a large pack of pre-cooked meatballs.

Long wooden walkways criss-cross Storön, the biggest island in the group. These have been strategically placed so you can reach any part, despite all the deep fissures and juniper thickets covering the island. It makes me think of Robinson Crusoe, jungle shacks and the art of moving through unforgiving terrain.

It takes three to four hours to circumnavigate the island on foot, even though the distance between the northern and southern extremities is only a kilometre. You are climbing and jumping and traversing crevices and boulders. It's not a problem, Sarah says. Our bodies will stiffen up if we don't stay active.

Her words make me smile. She has three children, chickens busily pecking around, a dog and all the daily chores for this place—it's hard for me to believe she spends much time sitting down!

She leads the way to the old cemetery that now looks more like a peaceful meadow. No gravestones are visible, but a profusion of purple and white summer flowers flourish in the long grass. A drystone wall surrounds the cemetery, its large rocks fitted together in a way that is reminiscent of ancient cairns. The hands that built this were experienced, I reflect as I touch the thin layer of moss covering the stones. They make me think of callused fists and physical strength.

Sarah stops at the old wooden bell tower.

"All our children were baptised here," she says, a softness in her eyes. "Fifty years ago, there was almost no sign of a cemetery—it was like a potato patch. There was no bell tower and no graves visible. But a priest from Blidö came to re-consecrate the ground to restore its status."

Sarah smiles, patting the dark wooden structure. The sun glints on the metal cross on top. A sudden gust bends the slim stalks of the bluebells in front of the wall.

"Everything's back to normal now. We've even had a few weddings out here."

On the north side of the island, the landscape is flatter, with small heather meadows, ancient rock carvings and old stone mazes on the flat rocks, said to be from the Middle Ages. Negotiating a maze without touching a single stone is said to bring a fisherman luck.

I enter a maze and walk round and round until I get to the middle, recalling that I have seen the same thing on other islands, where other equally patient predecessors have laid out similar stone formations.

They're like exquisite archipelago art installations, but also food for reflection.

After a while we return to the boat moored in the inner harbour, well sheltered from the wind. Sarah waves goodbye and I just make it into the boat without being attacked by the birds. I cast off with my hood pulled over my head. The terns screech in triumph as I leave Svenska Högarna behind me.

When dusk falls, the lantern lights up at the top of the lighthouse.

Next page: the only buildings in the Svenska Högarna group are on the main island, Storön. Lighthouse keepers have lived here since the 1800s. Wooden walkways lead you over hollows and crevices.

THREE SMÖRREBRØD

ROAST BEEF WITH DIJONNAISE, HORSERADISH AND EGG YOLK

- 1 slice dark whole grain or Pumpernickel
- 1 tbsp mayonnaise
- 1 tsp Dijon mustard
- 2 thin slices of cold roast beef
- 1 tbsp grated fresh horse-radish
- 1 egg yolk
- 3 pickled onions
- 3 Cornichons or small pickled gherkins
- finely chopped parsley

BUCKLING WITH KARTOFFEL

- 1 slice dark whole grain or Pumpernickel bread
- butter
- ¼ buckling or kipper
- 1 boiled new potato
- 1 tbsp Gravlax sauce or sweet mustard dressing
- 1 tsp capers
- 2 tsp finely chopped red onion
- 2 tsp finely chopped chives
- 2 radishes

MATJES HERRING WITH CHOPPED EGG

- 1 slice dark whole grain or Pumpernickel bread
- butter
- 1 matjes herring fillet (cut in two if it's too large)
- 1 tbsp crème fraîche or sour cream
- 1 tbsp Swedish cod roe spread (ideally non-smoked). Can be substituted with whitefish caviar
- ½ hard boiled egg
- dill

The Danes really know how to make a filling open sandwich, the famous smörrebrød! *This is perfect for lunch or the picnic basket. If you want to prepare ahead of time, store these in the fridge on a moistened tea towel and covered by plastic film (4–5 hours at most).*

The Danes like remoulade sauce with their roast beef sandwiches but surely Dijon mustard works just as well?

Here's how

Roast beef with Dijonnaise, horseradish and egg yolk:
Mix the mayonnaise and Dijon mustard and spread it on the bread. Grate the horseradish. Start with a lettuce leaf and add the rest of the ingredients on top. Finish off with the horseradish and make a little dent for the egg yolk.

Buckling with kartoffel:
Butter the bread. Clean the smoked fish from bones and skin. Slice the potato. Mix the sauce or dressing with the capers, onion and chives, reserving some chives for the garnish. Layer in this order: potato, fish and sauce. Garnish with thinly sliced radishes and chives.

Matjes herring with chopped egg:
Butter the bread. Drain the herring. Combine crème fraîche and the roe or caviar spread. Chop the egg. Place the herring on the bread and top off with crème fraîche, chopped egg and dill.

FISH EN PAPILLOTE, ISLAND STYLE

Serves 4:
800 g / 1 ¾ lb cod loin (or your fish of choice) cut into portion size
½ fennel bulb
2 carrots
½ leek
½ organic lemon
8–12 cherry tomatoes
salt
freshly ground black pepper
fresh dill
50 g / 2 oz butter
4 sheets of baking paper

An easy and healthy fish dish with rich flavours of fennel, tomato and lemon. It's great both for weekday dinners and for guests.

It's fun to open individual packets but it can also be made in a big oven dish, covered in baking paper. Just add an extra 10 minutes to the cooking time.

Here's how

1. Preheat the oven to 150C/300F. Peel and slice the fennel, carrots and leek paper thin. Wash and thinly slice the lemon, cut the tomatoes in halves.
2. Put a piece of fish in the middle of the paper. Lightly season with salt and pepper and place the vegetables, tomato, lemon slice and dill on top. Finish off with a few small dabs of butter and carefully fold the edges of the paper to create an "airy" parcel.
3. Bake the parcel in the middle of the oven for 15–20 minutes. It's practical to use a digital thermometer. The fish is done at 50–52C/120–125F. It's essential that the steam doesn't escape, partly because it cooks the vegetables and partly because the liquid makes a fantastic sauce.
4. Serve with riced potatoes or rice and the pesto.

DILL PESTO
Serves 4:
2 dl / ⅘ cup finely chopped dill
½ dl / ¼ cup peel almonds
1 clove of garlic
1 dl / ⅖ cup olive oil
½ dl / ¼ cup grated Parmesan or Västerbotten cheese

Dill is so summery. This is a classic recipe for pesto but with dill substituted for basil. This pesto will work well as an accompaniment to gravlax.

Here's how

Blend the dill, almonds and garlic in a food processor. Add the olive oil and grated cheese last. If saving for another day, cover the surface with a thin layer of olive oil. Stored in the fridge, it will last at least a week.

BREAKFAST ROLLS

Makes 20 rolls:
8 dl / 3 ⅓ cups plain flour
½ dl / ¼ cup wheat germ
1 tsp honey
1 tsp salt
100 g / ¼ lb butter
25 g / 8 oz fresh yeast or
2 ½ tsp active dried yeast
3 dl / 1 ¼ cups cold milk
1 egg

For glazing: buttermilk
1 tbsp wheat germ (can be excluded)

Isn't fresh-baked bread for breakfast wonderful? Especially when the closest bakery is many nautical miles away.

These rolls are ready-risen, waiting in the fridge for you to bake them for only 10 minutes.

Put the dough in muffin trays or on cutting boards so you can store them in the fridge.

Here's how

Evening day 1:

1. Pulse flour, wheat bran, honey, salt and butter in a food processor to make a crumbly dough.
2. Crumble the fresh yeast into a bowl with the milk (the milk should be cold). Stir until the yeast dissolves. Add the egg and the crumbly dough and knead until smooth.
3. Roll the dough into a snake and cut into 20 pieces. Place the rolls on a baking tray or ovenproof dish lined with baking paper. Dust with flour and cover with a tea towel. Let rise in the fridge overnight.

Morning day 2:

1. Preheat the oven to 225C/435F. Brush the rolls with buttermilk and dust with wheat germ.
2. Bake in the middle of the oven for about 10 minutes.

PALLARES
SOLSONA

SPRING VEGETABLES & FLAVOURED BUTTER

Serves 4:
4 golden or choggia beetsa
8 new potatoes
1 bunch fresh Summer carrots
1 bunch red spring onions
250 g / ½ lb green asparagus
1 bunch radishes

BASIL LEMON AND BUTTER
200 g / ⅓ lb unsalted butter at room temperature
small bunch of basil
1 organic lemon
flaked sea salt

The summer's tastiest veggies make a colourful splash that will light up any dinner table. Here, they're served with fluffy butter flavoured with lemon and basil.

It's a dish that will work on its own or as an accompaniment to meat or fish.

Here's how

1. Basil and lemon butter: Beat the butter with a fork until white and porous. Cut the basil into thin strips and grate the zest of the lemon. Combine butter, salt, lemon zest and basil. Keep the butter refrigerated but make sure to bring it to room temperature about 30 minutes before serving.
2. Trim and peel the vegetables. Wash the beets thoroughly but boil them with the skin left on (they're easier to peel when cooked).
3. Boil the beets in salted water for about 30 minutes. Boil the potatoes in lots of salted water. Add the carrots and onions for the last 5 minutes and the asparagus for the last 3 minutes of cooking time.
4. Slice the beets and halve the red onions. Trim and wash the radishes. Present all the vegetables on a pretty serving platter. Serve the tasty butter in individual bowls.

SARAH'S GARDEN TEA

Makes 6–8 glasses:
1 litre / 2 pints chilled tea, e.g. rooibos or green tea
2 limes
1 lemon
1 ½ dl / ⅔ cup cane sugar
100 ml / ½ cup dark rum
100 ml / ½ cup vanilla vodka
40 ml / ⅕ cup Cointreau
8 strawberries
2 dl / ⅘ cup mixed berries, preferably frozen, e.g. raspberries, blueberries and blackberries

This refreshing drink is cooling after a "tough" day of working in the garden. The only problem is that you might remain sitting down and not get up all evening, calling for more …

Garden tea can be served without alcohol if you prefer. Just substitute with orange juice.

Here's how

1. Squeeze the juice from 1 lime and 1 lemon into a large jug. Combine tea and sugar until dissolved.
2. Add rum, vodka and Cointreau. Stir.
3. Wash and cut 1 lime into thin slices. Layer fruit, berries, lemon balm and ice in a large jug and pour over the liquid. Serve immediately.

SALMON WITH HORSE-RADISH POTATOES

Serves 4:
800 g / 1 ¾ lb salmon or whitefish fillets cut into 4 portions
1 tsp neutral rapeseed oil
1 tsp salt
2 tsp sugar
a pinch of freshly ground white pepper

HORSERADISH-CREAMED POTATOES:
600 g / 1 ¼ lb freshly boiled and cooled new potatoes
1 dl / ⅖ cup crème fraîche or sour cream
1 dl / ⅖ cup thick yogurt
1 tbsp honey
1 tsp Dijon mustard
3 tbsp finely grated fresh horseradish
1 punnet garden cress
salt
freshly ground black pepper

This is so yummy I'm almost at a loss for words!

The velvety fish with its almost caramelised surface is a fantastic counterpoint to the sharp horseradish-creamed potatoes. A summer dish de luxe that is also a tempting sight.

Here's how

1. Brush the fillets with a thin layer of oil. Pat them with salt, sugar and white pepper to coat.
2. Heat a frying pan until really hot. Sear the fish quickly on each side until nicely charred. The fish should still have a raw centre. Be careful not to burn it.
3. *Horseradish-creamed potatoes:* If the potatoes are big, cut them in half. Combine crème fraîche, yogurt, honey, mustard and horseradish. Mix the cress (reserving some for the garnish) and the potatoes in the sauce. Season with salt and pepper.
4. Serve the fish with a lemon wedge and the horseradish-creamed potatoes topped with cress. If in season and available, garnish with dill weed flowers.

Remember:

If possible use a cast iron frying pan for this dish. Some non-stick pans cannot be heated to the degree needed without damaging the non-stick coating.

CRAYFISH PARTY ON SANDHAMN

CELEBRATING WITH FRIENDS AND SEAFOOD

With Sandhamn bathed in late summer sun, my thoughts turn to crayfish. Suddenly I begin to dream of dill, spiced cheese and rye bread. It's time for a crayfish party with the small freshwater crustaceans (resembling small lobsters) that are cherished by Swedes as the ultimate delicacy.

We usually set the table in front of the boatshed on the jetty. We grab all the chairs we can find in the house; the one at the end of the jetty is so close to the edge that we have to secure it with rope.

The colour theme is blue and white, with sturdy earthenware plates and pretty, though tarnished, silver cutlery. I knot the napkins with tarred twine (for the scent) and fill the vases with wildflowers. Then I pick through all the nooks and crannies in our old archipelago home for things I can use at the party. Mismatched *schnapps* glasses with elegant embellishments; a huge silver tray that makes a stylish bed for the crayfish; an ancient baby's bathtub in zinc that we fill with seawater to keep the *schnapps* and beer bottles chilled.

Setting a table on the jetty involves a lot of fetching and carrying. Everything has to be brought from kitchen to table, sometimes in baskets, sometimes piled high on trays. A summer on the island gives you muscles, let me tell you! But it's wonderful to sit outdoors by the water.

This isn't usually a problem (touch wood!) but there have been memorable exceptions. I remember one Midsummer's Eve when we broke all of our neighbour's *schnapps* glasses. One false step on a slippery rock surface was all it took, and glasses and their carrier wound up in a heap.

It hasn't stopped us carting china to the jetty.

There is something very special about a crayfish party. The mere sight of a table groaning under dishes of red crayfish, cheese and Västerbotten cheese pies makes me so happy. The crayfish liquor gives off an aroma that hovers above the table, there's chatter and laughter when the dishes

Sandhamn in the moonlight. To the right is the famous hotel built in 1897 as a clubhouse for the Royal Swedish Yacht Club. Today it serves hotel guests and conferences year-round.

are passed around. Everybody digs in with outstretched arms, piling their plates high.

"Let the slurping begin!" my husband calls out with gusto.

Lennart comes from Gothenburg on the west coast and loves all seafood, but especially crayfish. And he adores his own home-infused *schnapps*.

Ever since spring he's been keeping an eye on the big grey-green wormwood plant (*Artemisia absinthium*) growing outside the neighbour's fence. When it's properly bushy and luxuriant, he carefully picks a few fine sprigs for the schnapps (with the kind permission of our neighbour). He gently pushes the wormwood into an old apothecary bottle and adds potato vodka.

Put the wormwood sprigs in first, then the potato vodka (or regular vodka like Absolut). Seal and store for about four weeks. Dilute with more vodka to taste—one part concentrate to three parts vodka is a rule of thumb.

The more bitter the better, if Lennart has his way. Sometimes the taste is so sharp that I pull a wry face, making him laugh. When he's not looking, I prefer to fill up my glass with some store-bought Herrgårds Brännvin (flavoured with caraway, coriander and fennel). At least I can swallow that without searing my throat ...

Then the singing begins.

For the Sten family, singing traditional schnapps songs is compulsory. My beloved husband and I love to sing, and sing we do. We're happy to warble half the night away, if the guests or neighbours (or the children!) don't object.

It doesn't end until all plates are empty. (And there's still time to hum a tune with the coffee, if anybody feels inspired.)

There we are, replete and drowsy, gazing at the final flush of the setting sun. The flat sea is barely visible in the darkness. A full moon climbs the heavens. The dampness mists our glasses and there's a slight chill in the air. It's a bitter-sweet reminder that autumn is not far off. But the fun of our party helps us push away the thought of darker seasons.

In the August nights, there's still time for more dinners on the jetty, more food and laughter. In the archipelago, it's still summer.

An August night at its best. After a summer of food and friendships, a feeling of melancholy creeps in. But the archipelago is alive in both winter and summer—and it'll soon be summer again.

Next page: A crayfish party at dusk in the old marina together with the friends who have contributed to this book. The sun has just set and we're on our last *schnapps*—home-flavoured with bitter wormwood, of course!

SANDHAMN COCKTAIL

Makes 4 cocktails:
600 g / 1 ⅓ lb seedless watermelon
½–1 dl/ ¼–⅖ cup icing sugar (or to taste)
2 ½ dl / 1 cup Absolut Peach vodka
1 lemon, squeezed

A refreshing summer drink with a frozen margarita feel. The perfect way to kick off a party.

If you don't have watermelon you can freeze strawberries or raspberries. And if you don't have Absolut Peach vodka, any flavoured vodka will do. The point is to blend frozen fruit with flavoured vodka and a little icing sugar. Cheers!

Here's how

1. Cut the watermelon into large cubes and freeze for no less than 4 hours.
2. Combine the watermelon, icing sugar, spirits and lemon juice in a blender and blend into slush.
3. Serve immediately, semi-frozen.

HERB-INFUSED SCHNAPPS

WITH ST JOHN'S WORT OR WORMWOOD
Makes 1 small bottle:
St John's wort or wormwood
370 ml / approx. ½ pint vodka
+ more vodka to dilute according to taste

WITH DILL
Makes 1 small bottle:
4 large dillweed flowers
370 ml / approx. ½ pint vodka

What can be more tempting than a bottle of home-flavoured schnapps on the festive table? St. John's wort and wormwood both grow on Sandhamn. The sprigs should be picked before the plant blossoms. The milder St. John's wort is my favourite but my husband (a connoisseur) prefers wormwood. Bitter wormwood is his true love.

Here's how

1. Fill a 370 ml / approximately ½ pint bottle with flower of St John's wort (use only the flowers with seedpods), or wormwood (4–5 flowering sprigs). Fill up the bottle with vodka. Let it infuse for a minimum of 4 weeks for the concentrate to develop.
2. Dilute the concentrate to taste. About one part concentrate to three parts spirit is a rule of thumb. Add 1 sugar cube per 370 ml / approximately ½ pint mixed schnapps.

Dill-infused schnapps

Combine the dillweed and spirit in the bottle. Let it infuse overnight and remove the dillweed. Keep the schnapps chilled.

BAGUETTE & CREAM CHEESE

BAGUETTES
Makes 3 baguettes:
25 g / 1 oz fresh yeast or 2 ½ tsp active dried yeast
5 dl / 2 cups water
1 tbsp salt
13 dl / 5 ½ cups plain flour (approx. 800 g / 1 ¾ lb)

Tip
If you know you'll be pressed for time: mix the dough in a bowl in the morning and let it rise slowly in the fridge. Before the meal, tip the dough onto a baking tray and shape it into three long baguettes. Bake immediately.

CREAM CHEESE
Makes approximately 3 dl / 1 ¼ cups:
3 dl / 1 ¼ cups low fat sour cream (10%–12%)
1 dl / ⅖ cup finely chopped chives
salt
freshly ground black pepper

Few things say "welcome" like the smell of freshly baked bread. Ideally, serve these straight from the oven so that the butter will melt.

Here's how

1. Crumble the fresh yeast into a bowl. Heat the water to 37C/98F and dissolve the yeast in it. Add salt and most of the flour, reserving some for kneading.
2. Knead the dough forcefully until smooth. Let it rise under a cloth for about 1 hour.
3. Scoop it onto a flour-dusted work surface but do not knead.
4. Divide into three. Shape into long, thin loaves and place onto baking trays lined with baking paper. Cut diagonal slits on top and dust with a little flour. Let rise again for about 30 minutes. Preheat the oven to 250C/480F.
5. Bake in the middle of the oven for about 30 minutes. Let cool uncovered on a wire rack.

My friends are always impressed by my homemade cream cheese. They don't know how easy it is! A little sour cream, a coffee filter and a handful of fresh herbs are all you need. If you don't have chives handy, thyme will do, but use only half the amount in that case.

Here's how

1. Pour the sour cream into a coffee filter and let it drain for a few hours.
2. Scoop the drained cream cheese into a bowl and mix in the chives.
3. Season with salt and pepper. Let it rest in the fridge for at least an hour before serving.

EMILIE'S MUM'S CRISPBREAD

Makes approximately 12 pieces:
1 dl / ⅖ cup sunflower seeds
1 dl / ⅖ cup sesame seeds
½ dl / ¼ cup linseed
2 dl / ⅘ cup chickpea flour or cornflour
½ tsp sea salt
½ dl / ¼ cup olive or rapeseed oil
2 ½ dl / 1 cup boiling water

Ask my daughter, and she'll say this is the best crispbread ever, both crunchy and crisp. I often eat it with only lightly salted butter but it is divine with a slice of matured cheese. And it also works as a snack with drinks if you break it into small pieces and serve with cheese cubes.

1. Preheat the oven to 150C/300F. Combine all ingredients except the water in a large bowl. Add the boiling water and stir into a loose batter.
2. Line a baking tray with baking paper and spread the batter over the entire tray.
3. Bake the crispbread in the middle of the oven for just over an hour.

LENNART'S HOMEMADE MAYONNAISE

Makes approximately 3 dl / 1 ¼ cups:
2 egg yolks
½ lemon, squeezed
1 tsp white wine vinegar
½ dl / ¼ cup neutral rapeseed oil
salt
freshly ground black pepper

My dear husband believes that store-bought mayonnaise is a disgrace. In summer there's always a jar of his homemade kind in the fridge. He loves it on bread with tomato slices on top—what we call Lennart's Summer Sandwich. It's also devastatingly good with all kinds of shellfish.

Here's how

1. Beat egg yolks, lemon juice and vinegar in a bowl.
2. Add the oil in a thin steady stream, constantly whipping. Beat until smooth.
3. Season with salt and pepper.

GREEN SALAD

Serves 4–6:
2 heads of green lettuce
4 tomatoes
1 punnet of garden cress
olive oil
crema di balsamico
flaked sea salt
freshly ground black pepper
Optionally, toasted sunflower or pumpkin seeds

To the delight of the family, my father has dug a kitchen garden on Sandhamn. He grows lettuce, tomatoes and lots of herbs. He also has a greenhouse with delicacies like yellow squash, aubergines and cucumbers—both ecological and charming.

I often sprinkle salads with toasted seeds—sunflower or pumpkin, for example—for extra taste and to make it more filling.

Here's how

1. Rinse and roughly chop the lettuce.
2. Cut the tomatoes into chunks and mix with the cress and lettuce.
3. Drizzle oil and balsamico on top. Season with salt and pepper.

CHEESE PIE, BLACK & RED

Makes 8–10 pieces:
Crust:
3 dl / 1 ¼ cups plain flour
½ tsp salt
125 g / ¼ lb butter, cold
1 egg
1 tbsp ice cold water if needed

Filling:
3 eggs
2 ½ dl / 1 cup cream
1 dl / ⅖ cup milk
300 g / ¾ lb grated Västerbotten or Parmesan cheese
½ tsp salt
a pinch of freshly ground black pepper

Garnish:
1 jar red lumpfish caviar (80 g / 3 oz)
1 jar black lumpfish caviar (80 g / 3 oz)
2 dl / ⅘ cup crème fraîche or sour cream
small bunch of fresh dill

Sweden's Västerbotten cheese adds an unbeatable flavour to cheese dishes. I love this pie, where the combination of crème fraîche and lumpfish caviar balances the hearty cheese taste. The pie is filling and still there's enough for a feast, and leftovers the next day are almost more delicious.

Here's how

1. Crust: Combine flour and salt, cut the butter into pea size pieces and add to the flour. Add the egg and swiftly knead into a dough. If needed add 1 tbsp ice cold water. Press the dough into a pie plate about 24cm/10in in diameter. Let it rest in the fridge for 30 minutes. Preheat the oven to 200C/390F.
2. Prick the bottom with a fork and pre-bake the crust in the middle of the oven for 10–15 minutes.
3. Filling: Whip up eggs, cream and milk. Add the grated cheese. Season with salt and pepper.
4. Pour the filling into the pie crust and bake low in the oven for 25–30 minutes. The pie is done when the filling no longer wobbles when shaken and the top is nicely golden brown.
5. Garnish the top of the pie with crème fraîche, dollops of black and red caviar, and sprigs of dill. Serve luke-warm.

GRANNY SASCHA'S RED CURRANT CRUMBLE

Serves 6–8:
4 dl / 1 ¾ cups fresh red currants
100 g / ¼ lbs butter
1 ½ dl / ⅔ cup plain flour
2 dl / ⅘ cup sugar

Serve with:
vanilla ice cream or whipped cream

This is a recipe I inherited from my cherished grandmother who lived to be almost a hundred and one. I have been making this pie all my life and every time I take a first bite, I think of her. The tart currants are a perfect contrast to the sweet, crunchy topping with its slight crème brûlée feel.

Here's how

1. Preheat the oven to 250C/480F.
2. Grease a pie plate, approximately 24cm/10in in diameter and cover the bottom with currants.
3. Pinch butter, flour and sugar into large crumbs and spread on top.
4. Bake the crumble in the middle of the oven for 12–15 minutes until the top is golden and you have a beautiful crispy crust. Serve with ice cream or whipped cream.

Tip

This is equally delicious with other tart berries. I use blueberries as often as rhubarb. A fun combination is both currants and blueberries.

WHITEFISH CAVIAR ON SOURDOUGH TOAST

Serves 4:
4 Whitefish roe sacs
½ tsp salt
2 tsp Cognac
4 slices of sourdough bread
butter
2 dl / 1 cup crème fraîche or sour cream
1 dl / ⅖ cup finely chopped chives
4 thin lemon slices

This is the Sandhamn version of the classic Swedish vendace roe toast, but with my homemade whitefish caviar. Whitefish roe is lighter in colour but is just as good as vendace roe. Sourdough is extra good for the toast if it's handy. When I get to choose the starter, this is what I always make!

Here's how

1. Freeze the roe sacs for a minimum of 24 hours.
2. Remove from the freezer and thaw. With your hands, break the roe sacs under cold water. Discard any visible membrane or blood vessels. Carefully stir with a whisk so that any membrane and impurities stick to the whisk. Let the roe drain in a coffee filter for 30 minutes.
3. Transfer to a bowl and add ½ tsp salt or according to taste. Add 2 tsp Cognac, or more. Let it rest for at least an hour in the fridge before serving.
4. Cut the sourdough bread into 4 slices. Fry them golden brown in butter.
5. Arrange the roe on the toast. Garnish with a little crème fraîche, half a lemon slice and finely chopped chives. Schnapps and lager go with this beautifully!

WILD DUCK WITH RÖSTI & CHANTERELLES

Serves 4:
6–8 wild duck (mallard) breasts
8 medium sized potatoes
400 g/ 1 lb chanterelles
200 g/ ½ lb snow peas
butter
salt
freshly ground black pepper

Sauce:
4 dl / 1 ¾ cups red wine
1 tbsp beef stock
pinch of dry thyme
2 dl / ⅘ cup thick cream
1 tsp dark soy sauce
1 tbsp cornstarch + 2 tbsp water
salt
freshly ground black pepper

To serve:
snow peas tossed in butter

When summer is approaching its end, Swedes get the urge to find a forest and pick wild mushrooms. Summer chanterelles marry beautifully with the tart, game taste of wild duck breast in red wine sauce.

Served with Rösti (a big family favourite) this is a real feast. We have this when my husband has been shooting ducks.

Here's how

1. Start with the sauce: Reduce wine, beef stock and thyme by half in a small pot. Add thick cream and soy sauce. Boil over low heat for about 5 minutes. Thicken the sauce with cornstarch mixed with water. Season with salt and pepper.
2. Grate the potatoes on the rough side of the grater. Heat butter in a pan and with your hands shape the grated potato into a large pancake right in the pan. Season with salt and pepper and fry over medium heat for about 5 minutes before flipping it and frying another 5 minutes.
3. Trim the mallard breasts and remove any shot. Season with salt and pepper. Fry in plenty of butter until golden brown on the outside and slightly pink on the inside—about 5 minutes on each side.
4. Trim and wash the chanterelles and halve them by pulling them apart. Fry in plenty of butter until crisp. Season with salt.
5. Blanch the snow peas and toss them in butter. Serve the mallard with Rösti, sauce, chanterelles and snow peas.

ISLAND COOKING TIPS

These tips from me and my friends might simplify cooking when you don't have access to a fully equipped kitchen. Perhaps we could call it updated, old-fashioned know-how.

STRING BAG IN THE WATER

A string bag submerged in the water is the perfect cooler for sealed jars and bottles. It works for picnics or by your own jetty if you need cold beer for lots of guests.

BAKE-OFF FOR UNEXPECTED GUESTS

Make a sweet dough (for example the cinnamon bun recipe on page 102). Let the dough rise for 30 minutes and shape the buns in the usual way. Freeze them immediately. You can put them on a plastic cutting board and place the whole thing in the freezer. As soon as they're frozen (usually after about two hours) put them in a plastic bag and seal. They will keep for at least a month in the freezer.

When you need fresh buns, thaw for 1–2 hours on a baking tray. Bake as usual at 225C/435F for 5–10 minutes in the middle of the oven.

SWEET CRISPROLLS

Cut left-over buns into thick slices, brush with a little butter and sprinkle with sugar and cinnamon. Bake in the oven at 200C/390F for about 20 minutes. Allow to cool in the oven with the oven door slightly open. Store dry in a jar with a lid and they'll keep crisp and tasty for a long time.

REFRIGERATION, LYGNA STYLE

Place an old crate or similar in a shaded spot—a shed or outhouse, for example. Fill the crate with coarse salt to a depth of about 25cm/10in. You can keep butter, milk and cheese on top of the salt for weeks without spoiling, and they will stay cool. You can re-use the salt next year; just make sure the depth stays the same.

GROWING POTATOES IN KELP

Gather a big bunch of brown kelp slightly decayed (almost rotten at best). Push your seed potatoes deep into the kelp and leave them. Water once in a while, ideally with seawater so they won't need to be salted later on.

After 5–6 weeks it's time to dig the potatoes out. They are ready if they're smooth and shiny. They don't even need scrubbing before boiling.

KEEPING BOILED POTATOES WARM

Wrap the potato pot in old newspaper. It's a super idea for when you need to take potatoes with you for a picnic lunch on an island.

CLEANING BLUE FINGERS

Fingers blue from picking blueberries? Dilute household bleach—1 tsp bleach to 1 dl / ⅖ cup hot water—and dip your fingertips in the mixture for a minute or so. Voilà! Blue stains gone!

PICNIC IN A SMARTER WAY

- Take plastic bottles instead of glass. They weigh less and won't shatter if dropped on a hard surface like rock. A small bottle is also perfect for those who like milk with their coffee.
- Make a wrap of everything and you won't need cutlery. Think wraps and stuffed pancakes.
- Mugs are easier to pack than bowls, unless you prefer to use plastic bags. I usually fill big mugs with carrot and cucumber sticks or small cookies that would otherwise crumble.
- It's a good idea to bring along a roll of kitchen towel or toilet paper. Wipes are also useful.
- Pack an extra bottle of water, it'll always be appreciated.

WORDS AT TWILIGHT

MY ARCHIPELAGO AND YOURS

In the autumn of 2012, I bumped into well-known publisher and photographer Jeppe Wikström at Fotografiska, the museum of photography in Stockholm. It was purely by chance—or was it?

We are both archipelago aficionados and both of us have depicted the archipelago in our work for years, one through pictures, the other in crime novels.

We should do something together, we mused. And right there and then, this book was born.

Working on *Swedish Summer* has been a joy—sometimes going off a boat looking for early morning light, sometimes braving choppy waters late at night. Calm seas would lead us to narrow inlets and flocks of seabirds would appear in the warm evening sun.

The voyage took us from the lush vegetation of the inner archipelago to the bare rocks of the outer skerries. So much laughter, so much talk of food, and such wonderful cooking!

However, this hasn't just been about recipes and kitchen lore; we also talked about the archipelago, about old wisdom and new experience, about the future of this very special landscape.

The transformation of the archipelago over the last hundred years from self-sufficiency to tourism and service has been overwhelming. Traditions die as others are born. Change is unavoidable—seldom simple, sometimes painful.

There are concerns. What will happen when the seabird population drops dramatically, the Baltic sea becomes increasingly polluted and the residents face new challenges simply to make a living?

To remain islanders, the new generation has to find fresh sources of income. The longing for another life, in harmony with sea and nature, needs to be manifested in a way that fits modern society.

In many ways, the meeting point between old and new is exemplified by the people you have met in this book.

The true islander can tell his position from the swell of the sea, but he also uses GPS. Old tricks for storing perishables pre-electricity are even better when supplemented by solar cell technology. Ancient fishing techniques are reinvented in team-building seminars—nowadays seal hunts are conducted with lenses rather than bullets.

There's one thing that links all the contributors: their deep love for life in the islands, plus a commitment that takes nothing for granted. Nothing comes for free, especially if you're dedicated to preserving one of the world's most beautiful archipelagos.

A living archipelago needs helpers—from summer visitors recycling their rubbish to entrepreneurs identifying new opportunities. I often think about this. What can I as an individual contribute?

"Nobody can do everything but everybody can do something" is a good motto, whether we're talking about environment or lifestyles.

It's your archipelago and mine. But it's our shared responsibility.

INDEX

ALPHABETICAL

SUBJECT

BAKING

DESSERT

DRINKS

FISH

VEGGIE

MEAT

MISCELLANEOUS

THANKS

Many people have contributed to *Swedish Summer* and there are many to thank now that the book is done.

First and foremost, my friends from the islands for having so generously shared their time and lovely recipes: Janne Olsén, Eva & Klara Ejemyr, Erik Lindström, Fredrik Sjöblom, Magdalena Rinaldo and Sarah Anderin. My dear friends, it was such a pleasure visiting each one of you!

A warm thank you to Ewa Wrede, who kept a close check on the food, recipes, ingredients and everything else, and to Susanne Reali who patiently guided the project from start to finish.

Superb food stylist Tove Nilsson cooked the recipes and skilful food photographer Lina Eriksson took the wonderful food pictures. Thank you both so much. (Remember how pleased the neighbours were because we had to test everything in my kitchen on Sandhamn!).

Thank you, all my friends on Sandhamn who arranged coffee breaks, raised flags for the pictures, lent us props and helped out in all kinds of ways.

Finally, I'd like to thank my publisher, Jeppe Wikström, for steering this book through whilst taking the fantastic scenic pictures. And thanks to everyone else at Bokförlaget Max Ström who worked on *Swedish Summer*: Simon, Patric and Amelie.

Last but not least—thanks to my beloved gourmet husband Lennart, who shared his favourite recipes and helped with the cooking whenever we ran into trouble.

Sandhamn, 27 March, 2014.
Viveca Sten

Angsö
Vettershaga
Yxlan
Östanå
N. Ljusterö
Gälnan
S. Ljusterö
Ingmarsö
Svartsö
Trälhavet
Saxar-
fjärden
Vaxholm
Grinda
Askrikefjärden
Lidingö
Vindö
Kanholms-
fjärden
Värmdö
Saltsjö-
baden
Stavsnäs
Runmarö
Ingarö
Tyresö
Nämdöfjärden
Nämdö
Mörtö
Dalarö
Jungfrufjärden